THAT'S NOT WHAT I SAID

Master Conflict with

Conversational Competence

DETHRA U. GILES

3G Publishing, Inc.
Loganville, Ga 30052
www.3gpublishinginc.com
Phone: 1-888-442-9637

First published by 3G Publishing, Inc. August, 2025.

ISBN: 9781956382099

Printed in the United States of America

Contents

Thank You

First and always, thank You, God—for the vision, the voice, and the framework. The DARE model wasn't just a good idea. It was a divine assignment. Thank You for trusting me with it, for guiding my steps (even when I questioned them), and for being the constant when everything else felt like chaos.

To my husband, Frank Giles—my rock, my calm, my covering. Thank you for loving me through deadlines, rewrites, early mornings, and late nights. Your belief in me, even when I'm doubting myself, is the wind behind every bold move I make.

To my favorite daughter, Jairah Giles, and my favorite son, Daniel Giles—you two are my greatest reasons. Thank you for being the kind of people who make me proud to be your mother. Your curiosity, brilliance, and love inspire everything I do.

To my mother, Margaret Terri Daniels—you planted the seeds of strength, wisdom, and audacity in me long before I ever put them on paper. Thank you for being my first example of excellence, and for showing me that my voice mattered before the world ever echoed it back.

And to every single person who supported me, cheered for me, prayed for me, edited chapters, listened to rants, reminded me to eat, or simply said "you've got this"—thank you. This book was not written alone. It is the result of community, love, and the kind of support that wraps around a dream and makes it real.

With deepest gratitude

Dethra Giles

Introduction: The Conversations You're Avoiding Are Costing You

The High-Stakes Conversation That Almost Ruined Everything

It was supposed to be a simple dinner among friends. One of those rare moments when everyone's crazy schedules aligned, and we all sat around the table, plates full, laughing about something completely meaningless. And then, my friend Andre, who, bless his heart, has the subtlety of a bullhorn, decided to drop the question:

"So, what does everyone think about the election?"

Let's pause for a second. They say there are three things you should never bring up unless you're looking to start a fight—the three R's: Race, Religion, and Politics. Yes, I know politics starts with a P, but we're going with the three R's anyway. Remember how we accepted Reading, Writing, and Arithmetic as the three R's, and no one raised an eyebrow? The same logic applies.

Now, I don't actually believe those topics are off-limits. They matter too much, and discussing these topics with people of different opinions is healthy and needed. The problem isn't the topics themselves. The problem is that most people have never been taught how to handle the disagreement that usually follows. So instead of diving in with care and questions, they charge in with stance and statements, then act surprised when things blow up.

Things blew up in epic proportions around the 2024 U.S. Presidential election—I mean it felt like the country was walking around with a lit match and a gas can. Tensions were sky high. Families fractured over tweets, couples were separating, and longtime friends were calling it quits. People felt they couldn't speak freely about the election. First, they would test the waters. Throw out a vague meme or say something like, "The Democrats, am I right?" and wait to see what the person said.

7

If the person said something that indicated a shared political belief system? Congratulations, you had yourself a bonding moment and a safe space to rant. But if they didn't? You got the tight smile, the long pause, or worse, the look: sharp, silent, and screaming, "I thought I knew you."

So, to casually ask, "So, what does everyone think about the election?" at a peaceful weekend gathering designed for grilled food, slow music, and people pretending to forget they had inboxes?

Big sigh.

I swear, the question stopped time. Forks hovered in midair. Sheila adjusted in her seat like she was strapping in for turbulence. My best friend, who usually plays referee, gave me that look. The one who said, "You are the one trained in mediation. Fix it. Now."

There sat Andre, sipping his wine, after he'd just pulled the pin of a social grenade.

As expected, it exploded. Spectacularly.

One friend immediately launched into a passionate defense of their political stance. Another friend countered with a rebuttal so sharp it could have sliced the ham. Voices rose. Hands slammed on the table. It was so bad, the dog who lingered around the table hoping someone would drop food slowly backed away and out of the room.

Within minutes, a peaceful dinner had turned into a battleground. And the saddest part? No one was actually listening to each other. They were just waiting for their turn to talk– or worse, to win.

I sat there watching the carnage, thinking, This is why people hate talking about hard things. This is why so many of us avoid tough conversations entirely. We think the only two options are silence or war.

We avoid, deflect, misinterpret, and sometimes, despite our best intentions, escalate difficult conversations. And the cost to our relationships, homes, work, and communities is enormous.

According to a study by VitalSmarts, 72% of people report avoiding difficult conversations at work, and when they do engage, one in five employees say their anxiety about the conversation impacts their ability to be productive. Meanwhile, research from The Gottman Institute suggests that 69% of marital conflicts are never actually resolved– couples just argue about them repeatedly without a productive outcome.

And let's not get started on how social media has turned the art of conversation into a battlefield

But here's the thing: It doesn't have to be this way. There is a better way.

Why Conflict Feels Overwhelming and the Science Behind It

Arousal, the Brain, and Conflict: The Science Behind It

Here's a harsh truth: Most of us are bad at difficult conversations. Not because we're bad people, but because no one ever really taught us how to have them..

If conflict were a reality TV show, most of us would be watching it from behind our fingers, cringing at the tension and praying for a commercial break. Conflict makes people uncomfortable, plain and simple.

But why does it feel so overwhelming, and why do we avoid it like we would an ex we've blocked on all social media platforms? The simple answer is science.

Our brains are hardwired to react to conflict in the same way they register imminent danger. There is a biological reason for this response. When we sense disagreement, the amygdala, the part of the brain responsible for alerting us to potential dangers that may harm us, lights up like a Christmas Tree. The amygdala did a wonderful job keeping our prehistoric ancestors safe from predators, but it has yet to adapt to differentiate between an argument with a co-worker about heating up last night's fish dinner in the breakroom microwave and the shock of being startled by an angry bear during an otherwise pleasant nature hike. People often say we have three responses to fear, but really, we have three responses to *arousal*, and fear just happens to be one of them. I want to pause here for those of you who giggled at the word *arousal*. I'll let you have your moment. We listen and we don't judge… Welcome back.

Fear is a form of arousal, and our responses to arousal are fight, flight, freeze, and fawn.

9

Why do we panic when we're late? Why do we yell, go silent, or completely blank during conflict? Because arousal kicks in. Ever said "I was so mad I couldn't think"? Well, you were partly right, but your sentence was missing a word. You should have said: "I was so mad I couldn't think WELL."

Why? Because the well-thinking part of our brain took a break. (To all the neuroscientists reading this—I'm about to oversimplify this in a way that might make your eye twitch. But keep in mind: this is a book about conversational competence, not neuroanatomy.)

That well-thinking part of the brain is the prefrontal cortex. It handles planning, judgment, decision-making, impulse control, and—yes—language. When stress floods our system, this logical hub steps aside and lets the amygdala, part of the ancient limbic system, take the wheel.

That moment at the surprise party when everyone yells "SURPRISE"? Your first reaction is probably to pause, back away, or cover your mouth. That's your limbic system doing its job. It's the same system that tells a deer to freeze in front of headlights—because in the wild, standing still might mean camouflage. It's automatic. Instinctual. It requires no thinking.

And when you're in a heated conversation, your body doesn't know the difference between an angry spouse and a saber-toothed tiger.

Your amygdala lights up like a Christmas tree. Cortisol floods your system. Your brain shifts blood flow from the prefrontal cortex to your limbs so you can run or throw hands. It's survival mode.

This is why we forget basic words, why we can't articulate complex ideas, why we shut down, lash out, or go blank. Our brain literally prioritizes survival over communication in order to get us out of perceived danger.

Conflict, even minor conflict, can feel overwhelming, not because we're weak or overly sensitive, but because our biology is trying to protect us, even when there's no actual threat. Our nervous system interprets disagreement as danger, and before we even open our mouths, we're in defense mode.

So if you've ever walked away from a conversation thinking, *Why didn't I say that?* Or *why did I say that?!* Congratulations. You're human.

Conflict isn't just overwhelming; it triggers our body's physiological stress response of fight, flight, freeze, or fawn, making it harder to think rationally, listen effectively, and regulate our emotions.

Do you tend to react with fight, flight, freeze, or fawn in a conflict? My go-to response is fight. Now don't judge me because, like you, I learned my conflict style as a child from the adults in my life. I learned there were two options: shut down or act up, and acting up felt better for me.

I remember my first encounter with demonstrated conversational competence. I was a young college student, and my then-boyfriend, now husband, and I got into a disagreement. To this day, I don't remember what we were arguing about, but I remember the course of events as if it were yesterday. I was angry, and I went into my usual verbal fight response, complete with a sharp tone and defensive, sarcastic comebacks. He looked at me like I had two heads, and they were both spinning. Very calmly, he said, *"What are you doing?"* Shocked by the question, I immediately paused out of confusion and said, *"Huh, what do you mean, what am I doing?"*

He said, *"You just raised your voice at me. Why?"* Now, at this point, I was questioning everything—*Did he not know he did something to anger me? Does he not know how arguments work? Is he not as smart as I thought he was?* So, with genuine confusion, I said, *"We are arguing."* To that, he responded, *"Not like that. We don't yell at each other. We can disagree and not be disrespectful, and yelling at me is disrespectful."*

I put both hands under my chin and leaned in like a kindergartener at story time. I was intrigued—disagreeing without raising my voice, but how?

For many of us, our first exposure to conflict was watching our parents argue or avoid arguing. Maybe you grew up in a house where disagreements meant slammed doors and sharp, sarcastic quips. Or perhaps conflict was avoided altogether, only noted by tense silences, swept under the rug like dirt that no one wanted to actually clean up. These messages were reinforced as you picked up social and cultural cues at school, your first job, and in your friendships about what is safe to say and what is not.

Because of these formative experiences, we tend to develop two extreme approaches to conflict: avoidance or aggression.

Avoidance sets you up to dodge confrontation. You tell yourself, *It's not worth the fight. I don't want to make things awkward,* so *I'll just let it go, and it will fix itself.* But instead of going away, the issue festers, and resentment builds until you explode over something benign like your partner breathing too loudly.

On the other hand, aggression positions you to prepare for battle. You don't just bring up the problem; you bring all the evidence and an entire PowerPoint presentation. The goal isn't resolution, it's winning. And while you might feel a momentary victory, you often leave the other person defensive, hurt, and even less likely to hear what you're saying.

Spoiler alert: Neither of these strategies works. Avoidance breeds resentment while aggression breeds resistance. So, what's the alternative? Enter the D.A.R.E. model, a conflict communication strategy designed to help you shift from avoidance or aggression to effective engagement, staying grounded, guiding the conversation, and ultimately coming out with real, shared solutions.

The D.A.R.E. Model:

Your Superpower in Navigating Conflict

From Conflict to Conversational Competence

If you've ever wished there was a formula for making conflict feel less like a dumpster fire, this is where the **D.A.R.E. Model** comes in. It's not about avoiding difficult conversations or overpowering the other person. Instead, it's about competently navigating them with skill, clarity, and emotional intelligence. Instead of getting caught in the chaos, this model will teach you how to stay grounded, guide the conversation, and come out with real solutions.

The D.A.R.E. Model is a method for individuals to resolve conflicts without requiring a referee. It's built on four key principles:

1. **Describe vs. Interpret** – Because stepping back from what we made "it" mean gives us the clarity to move forward..

2. **Acknowledge Similarities Without Minimizing Differences** – Because similarities give us comfort, but differences are where the work begins.

3. **Review the Narrative(s) You've Accepted as Fact** – Because your "facts" may be wrong and your narrative outdated.

4. **Engage for Conversation, Not Conversion** – Because the only person you can change is you, with everyone else, you engage in conversation.

The D.A.R.E. Model will help you shift from avoidance or aggression to effective engagement, making conflict feel less like a battle and more like a bridge to better relationships and outcomes at work and home. I bet you're wondering how this model came to be; trust me, it involved some serious trial and error.

The Birth of the D.A.R.E. Model: The Day I Learned that Yelling Wasn't a Love Language

If conflict were an Olympic sport, my family would have taken home the gold, silver, and bronze. Growing up, I didn't witness "disagreements" so much as full-blown battle royales. I'm talking about shouting matches that could rival any UFC event. There was no *sitting* down calmly, saying, *Hey, let's talk about this rationally.* Oh no, we yelled. Everyone except my mother, who was

silent but deadly. She was a woman of action. And if the yelling didn't work, well, sometimes things escalated in ways that would make a video go viral.

I come from a long line of verbal gladiators. We didn't just raise our voices; we launched them, like missiles, directly at each other's egos. If you had the audacity to try to "win" an argument, good luck. You'd better come armed with solid talking points, a deep breath, and an athletic ability to dodge flying objects, not always metaphorically speaking.

I thought this was normal. I truly believed that if you weren't raising your voice, you had no passion for the topic, and if you have no passion, then why are we arguing?

And then I met my husband.

I told this story earlier, but it bears repeating. When I first started dating my now-husband, I thought he was *broken*. Seriously. We had our first real disagreement about something incredibly minor, probably about what to eat for dinner or the correct way to roll the toilet tissue. I was ready. I took a deep breath, squared my shoulders, and launched into battle mode, prepared to let my frustration fly.

While I stood strong, ready for him to give me his best, he didn't give me anything but a strange look.

Then, in the calmest, most unnervingly normal tone, he said, *"What are you doing?"*

Excuse me? Sir? That's how we do things around here. Welcome to the part of the relationship where we verbally step into the octagon. Put your gloves on and let's do this.

But he wouldn't. He simply shook his head and said, *"We don't yell at each other. We can disagree, but we're not going to do it like this."*

I wish I could say those words caused an immediate epiphany, I instantly understood and changed my ways, but no, my brain short-circuited. I had never encountered someone in my life who believed conflict could exist without volume. It was like someone casually telling me they don't breathe oxygen. *What do you mean, we don't yell? What are the other options?* This was a sincere question that I needed answered. I needed an answer so badly that I forgot what I was angry about and leaned in to hear the answer. I knew I didn't like screaming, yelling, or receiving verbal insults, but I also knew I wasn't a pushover. I was very comfortable stating my stance, defending it, and sticking to it.

Still, I desperately wanted to know how civility and disagreement could coexist in the same conversation.

That moment planted a tiny seed of doubt in my very loud, very argumentative heart. It made me wonder: *Is there another way?*

There is. And I was about to spend my entire career figuring it out.

From Chaos to Conflict Management: My Academic Journey

Realizing that not everyone operated in a constant state of verbal warfare shook me to my core. I decided I needed answers. So, like any self-respecting overachiever, I went out and earned a Master of Science in Conflict Management. Yes, folks. I took my family's dysfunction and turned it into a degree.

Some people inherit wealth, but I inherited an in-depth knowledge of how to fight effectively.

I did not stop there. I went even deeper. I studied mediation, with advanced training in divorce mediation, and eventually served as a mediator in actual divorce cases. Nothing will make you reevaluate the importance of communication like sitting between two people who once shared a life but are now arguing over the ashes of the dead cat. Getting the degree wasn't about adding additional accolades to my resumé. It was about undoing everything I thought I knew about conflict. I learned that yelling doesn't equal resolution, that most people argue based on emotions rather than facts, and that the majority of conflicts aren't about what they seem to be about. Hint: That couple fighting over leaving dishes in the sink? They're not fighting about dishes. They're fighting about being heard and feeling unappreciated.

The Divorce Table: Where It All Clicked

There's something surreal about watching people go from *"till death do us part"* to *"I will burn your house down before I let you have the dirty, roach-infested couch grandma gave us when we got married 15 years ago."* Divorce mediation reminded me of a child I once heard at a Little League event. He said very confidently, *"I can't win them all, but I can make you wish you'd lost."* In my decade of working with divorcees, I can say that was how most divorcing couples approached mediation.

I'd watched people argue for hours over things that had no value to the average person. I know you're thinking those things probably had sentimental value to them. Nope, this was something different. I sat in mediations where couples fought over who was going to pick up the kids from school, and it wasn't about the schedule; it was about lingering resentment from a fight that happened five years ago. These former partners battled over household furniture, as if they were on *Shark Tank*, not because they cared about the couch, but because the couch was a trophy awarded to the winner. There were times during mediation when I would remind the couples, *"Remember, you are paying by the hour. I am not complaining, but I want to be respectful of your time and money."*

But here's what struck me the most—**so many of these partnerships could have been saved**. Or at the very least, their divorces could have been

less messy, less painful, and way less expensive if someone had just taught them conversational competence.

I realized that people aren't just bad at resolving conflict, they're bad at even having it. They don't know how to communicate in a way that leads to resolution rather than resentment. And it hit me— if I could help people learn how to have better conversations, I could keep more relationships from falling apart, whether those were marriages, friendships, co-workers, project teams, or everyday workplace dynamics.

That realization didn't start ExecuPrep, but it sharpened my conviction about why the work we do matters. ExecuPrep was born out of my years in HR—watching brilliant professionals get stuck not because they lacked skill, but because they lacked the tools to navigate people, conflict, and culture.

Over time, it became clear: communication isn't just a soft skill—it's the operating system behind everything else. Promotions, partnerships, performance… all of it rises or falls on how well we communicate, especially when the stakes are high.

At ExecuPrep, we've taken that truth and built it into everything we do. Our coaching, training, and strategy sessions are infused with the D.A.R.E. Model, helping leaders and teams build real conversational competence— the kind that fosters trust, creates clarity, and drives meaningful results.

And here's what we've seen: when communication gets better, everything gets better. People perform at a higher level. Teams function more smoothly. Turnover slows. Conflict doesn't disappear—but it gets handled.

Because silence costs too much, and most tension doesn't come from what's said—it comes from what stays unspoken.

Since then, the ExecuPrep team has brought this approach into rooms around the world: boardrooms, break rooms, classrooms, courtrooms, and yes, even the occasional therapy-adjacent Zoom call. We've tested the D.A.R.E. Model with thousands of people and hundreds of leaders across high-stakes industries, multinational corporations, nonprofits, and leadership cohorts spanning five continents.

And here's what we've learned—regardless of country, title, or tax bracket, the ability to communicate clearly, especially when emotions are high, is a game-changer. In companies we've partnered with, teams report fewer stalled projects, faster decision-making, improved morale, and measurable gains in performance, productivity, and profit.

This approach works. It's why I was invited to deliver a TEDx Talk on the topic, and why the model continues to change conversations—and bottom lines—around the world.

I took everything I had learned—my upbringing, the yelling, the divorce mediation, the degrees, workplace disputes, and grocery line kerfuffles—and created a formula that makes difficult conversations easier.

Commercial Break

I want to take a commercial break right here and focus on a word I just used. Notice, I said **"make difficult conversations easier,"** emphasis on the "-ier" of *easier*. Easier is not to be confused with *easy*. The Pythagorean theorem doesn't make geometry easy; it makes it easier. That's what the D.A.R.E. Model does for conflict conversations. It increases your likelihood of success in a conflict conversation, which means you'll take more opportunities to engage. And that, my friend, is life-changing.

Back To The Program

The D.A.R.E. Model is my way of helping you navigate conflict on your own, even while being a little unsure, because the conversations we avoid or fumble are costing us more than we realize.

The Cost of Conflict: A Leadership and Communication Breakdown

Sarah wasn't just any developer: she was *the* developer.

Recruited straight out of a top-tier computer science program, she had quickly risen to become one of the company's most valuable team members. Her technical brilliance was matched only by her ability to solve complex problems and mentor junior developers. Leadership saw her potential early, investing more than $150,000 in specialized leadership development, project management training, and high-impact coaching. She was on the fast track to becoming a lead architect; maybe even a future VP of Engineering.

Yet, beneath the surface of her success, Sarah was drowning.

Her workload had steadily increased, and while she had always been the person who "figured it out," the weight of expectation was crushing. She hesitated to speak up, afraid that admitting struggle would make her seem weak. After all, she had been identified as a leader, someone others relied on. Saying, *"I need help,"* felt like failure. Her grandma always told her, *"You have to be five times better and never let them see you sweat while you do it."*

While Sarah hid it well, the signs were there. Her once-detailed code reviews started coming back with errors. She had a reputation for arriving early and was now showing up late to meetings. Her energized attitude was now drained. Deadlines came really close to being missed. Frustration built. But no one asked Sarah what was wrong, because she was still outperforming her counterparts.

And Sarah? She never said a word. She gave no indication she was drowning.

This wasn't just a failure of leadership; it was a failure of conversational competence on all sides.

Her manager noticed the shift in her performance but avoided asking hard questions. Sarah was still outperforming everyone else. And, what if Sarah felt insulted? What if she was just having a bad month? The discomfort of the conversation kept her manager silent.

Sarah's teammates sensed her frustration but assumed she would speak up if something were truly wrong. No one wanted to seem like they were prying, and let's be honest, no one wanted to take on her work if it was discovered that Sarah's tasks needed to be redistributed.

Sarah knew she was struggling, but didn't know how to say, *"I'm having a hard time, and I need help."* Even worse, she didn't know how to say, *"I have a disproportionate amount of work compared to everyone else."* She worried that making such declarations would change how people saw her and change her opportunities for advancement.

Everyone remained silent until the silence got very loud.

In the midst of a critical, $200 million project where Sarah was the lead, she gave two weeks' notice of her resignation. She quit!

Her resignation blindsided the company. Leadership scrambled to convince her to stay, but it was too late; burnout had already taken its toll. She was exhausted, disillusioned, and convinced she was no longer in an environment where she could thrive. What's worse, she wasn't leaving for another company or opportunity– she was leaving for a vacation; a break from it all.

The True Cost of Losing Sarah

The cost of losing Sarah was staggering:

- Recruitment Costs: Replacing her meant an extensive hiring process—job postings, recruiter fees, technical assessments, and multiple rounds of interviews, totaling nearly $40,000 before a new hire was even onboarded.

- Lost Productivity: It took six months to fill Sarah's position and another 2-3 months to train the new hire, causing key projects to be delayed and stretching her former team to their limits. The company lost an estimated $300,000 in project revenue during the first six months of her departure.

- Knowledge Drain: Sarah had built systems and processes no one else fully understood. Her departure left gaps that took nearly 18 months to fill.

- Wasted Leadership Investment: The $150,000 in leadership development? It walked out the door with Sarah, hopefully benefiting her next employer instead, but currently benefiting the beaches of Zanzibar.

In case you were doing the math, that is nearly half a million dollar loss, and all of it, Sarah's burnout, her departure, the financial impact, could have been avoided if leaders had the skill to ask the right questions, and if Sarah had the skill to answer honestly or advocate for herself. No one had the conversation, and Sarah didn't speak up because no one knew how to have the hard conversations.

Conversational competence isn't just a nice-to-have—it's the difference between retaining top talent and watching your investment in talent walk out the door.

Leaders Must Learn to Ask Tough Questions

"I've noticed that in the past few weeks, your code reviews have had more errors than usual, and you've been skipping lunch breaks. I also see that you've been working late most nights. Can you tell me what's going on?"

"Over the last month, I've seen you take on three major projects while still handling urgent bug fixes. I've also noticed you're responding to messages after hours. I want to make sure you have the resources you need. What would be most helpful right now?"

Sarah's story is real. I have changed the name and omitted the company's information so you can focus on the lesson, not the names. This is a lesson for leaders and employees alike: Silence does not indicate a lack of conflict. Quiet conflict is expensive, and honest conversations are priceless.

So, how many Sarahs are brewing in your company right now? How many are one day away from taking your investment in them to another company? More importantly, what conversations are you avoiding that could keep them?

The Ripple Effect of Avoiding Hard Conversations

Unspoken frustrations don't just lead to resignations; they create workplaces where dysfunction thrives. Sometimes, employees stay, but productivity erodes because tough conversations never happen.

A team member isn't pulling their weight, and yet:

- Everyone assumes the supervisor will step in.

- People hesitate, worried they'll come off as overstepping or difficult.

- No one wants to add another headache to their already full plate.

- Others begin to slack off, too, figuring if that team member can get away with it, maybe they can coast, too.

The result? Resentment builds, productivity declines, and silent frustration gives way to disengagement.

The Path Forward: Building a Culture of Conversational Competence

Organizations that fail to foster conversational competence pay the price, not just in turnover, but in wasted potential. A culture where employees feel empowered to address concerns directly, openly, and respectfully is a culture that retains talent, fosters collaboration, and ultimately drives results.

The question isn't whether these conversations will happen. It's whether they'll happen in time and in a way that makes a difference.

Why the D.A.R.E. Model Works

While we can't control our body's initial physiological reaction, we can train ourselves to manage it. Conversational competence is the ability to stay in the moment, manage emotional arousal, and communicate productively even when disagreement is on the table. It's knowing how to:

- Recognize your emotional triggers
- Slow yourself down (mentally and verbally)
- Use words that clarify, not escalate
- Shift from defensiveness to curiosity

The D.A.R.E. Model, a practical application of conversational competence theories, helps override the limbic system's panic by providing a framework. Why? Because structure lowers stress. Using structure over time stores it in the limbic system. Dr. Julia Minson, a conflict researcher at Harvard, found that people who actively practice perspective-taking are 40% more likely to de-escalate tension and reach mutual understanding. That's not magic, it's muscle memory. It's practice.

Structure tells your brain: *We've been here before. We know what to do.*

Each step **—Describe, Acknowledge, Review, Engage** —creates space for your brain to re-engage with logic, empathy, and clarity. Instead of reacting, you respond.

21

We're not here to eliminate conflict because that is not gonna happen. We're here to make it less overwhelming, more manageable, and infinitely more productive.

So, the next time you feel yourself about to scream "ya momma" in a meeting, or you forget how to form a complete sentence because your co-worker is tap dancing on your last nerve, remember: your brain isn't broken. It just needs a new strategy to navigate conflict effectively and productively.

How to Use This Book

Let's start with the truth: You've probably got at least one self-help, leadership, or communication book sitting on your nightstand, bookshelf, or Kindle right now... half-read and quietly judging you. Maybe you even bought the fancy highlighters, told your group chat you were "you'd found your next key to success," and then promptly forgot where you left off when you stopped reading.

No shame, we've all done it.

But this book? This book is not meant to collect digital dust or become a really expensive coaster. This one is designed for repeated use. This is not a communication textbook; it's a gym for your conversational muscles. And like any good gym, you get stronger the more you engage.

This book will not turn you into a conflict Jedi who floats into every tense conversation with sage-like wisdom and zero emotions. You will still be human. You're still going to get annoyed, frustrated, maybe even a little petty. Here is the worst part: you will still, on occasion, handle conflict in a way that does not make you proud.

However, it *will* provide you with the tools, language, and mindset to navigate those moments when there is a high potential for disagreement with greater clarity, control, and confidence.

This book is not:

- A lecture

- A guilt trip

- A "just stay calm and use 'I' statements" manual

- An "easy button"
- A read-it-and-forget-it-and-expect-results guide

This book is:

- Relatable – Real stories from real situations (many of which are mine and very human, though the names have been changed to protect the guilty, and company names have been left off to protect me from lawsuits).

- Research-backed – Anecdotal evidence is good, and anecdotal evidence backed by researched data reigns supreme. The goal is to provide you with the best information, as my clients call it: "University Tested and Industry Approved."

- Practical – Exercises you can use today and every day after.

- Fun – Because if we're going to talk about hard things, we might as well enjoy ourselves.

- Don't worry, there isn't a quiz at the end. But you *will* be challenged. And I promise, you'll come out better on the other side.

How the Book Is Designed

Each chapter is built around one part of the D.A.R.E. model:

- Describe vs. Interpret
- Acknowledge similarities without minimizing differences
- Review the narrative(s) you've accepted as fact
- Engage for conversation, not conversion

These are more than just cute words that fit nicely into an acronym. They are real, powerful practices that help you shift from reaction to intention.

Throughout the chapters, you'll find:

- Real-World Examples – Scenarios pulled from workplaces, homes, friend groups, and anywhere humans exist.

- Insights and Explanations – To help you understand why things go left in conversations and how to course correct.

- Conversation Starters – Actual phrases and prompts to try out in your next meeting, group chat, or family dinner.

- Practice Exercises – Quick activities to build your conversational competence muscle.

- Reflection Prompts – To help you check in with yourself. Because growth starts with awareness.

Pro tip: You don't have to read this book in order. If you're struggling with a particular part of a conflict (say, jumping straight to assumptions), jump to that chapter. This book is built to meet you where you are.

But whatever you do, *use* it. Mark it up. Highlight it. Dog-ear the pages. Argue with me in the margins if you need to. Write down questions you cannot wait to ask me when we meet. Just don't let it sit quietly on your shelf pretending to help you grow. Growth doesn't come from proximity to the information; it comes from engaging with it. I encourage you to buy a second or third copy. What you'll realize is that as you begin to master one area, you'll start to focus on another.

Who Should Use This Book

Everybody. This book isn't just for corporate leaders or HR managers. This book is for:

- The team lead navigating sticky dynamics with a high-performing but difficult employee

- The couple trying to figure out how to talk about money without yelling or walking away

- The sibling who hasn't spoken to their brother since that one Thanksgiving incident

- The friend who's tired of ghosting instead of setting boundaries

- The group chat member who types and deletes before hitting send because... tension

- And yes, the boss, the coworker, the parent, the pastor, the partner, the PTA president

If you are in any kind of relationship where human interaction is involved, otherwise known as *life*, this book is for you.

And let's be clear: conversational competence isn't just about avoiding conflict. It's about creating connections. It's about becoming someone others trust to be honest, fair, and emotionally intelligent, even when the conversation is uncomfortable.

A Personal Note from Me to You

This book is built on what I've learned from studying conflict academically, navigating it professionally, and surviving it personally.

There will be parts that make you laugh. Parts that make you wince. Parts that might make you text someone and say, "Hey, can we talk?" And that's all by design.

So here's my invitation:

Use this book as a toolkit. Not a checklist. Not a report card. A toolkit.

Return to it when:

- A hard conversation goes badly, and you're wondering what happened
- You feel misunderstood or misheard
- You're preparing for a conversation that makes your stomach flip
- You're tired of avoiding things that matter

Also, quick heads up, if you want to throw this book across the room at some point, just breathe. That just means you're growing. Lean into it. That discomfort? That's where the good stuff is.

Because you don't just *need* better conversations, you deserve them.

Let's D.A.R.E. to have them.

Part I

Executive Summary: The High Cost of Poor Conversations

Let's get honest: most of the conflict we experience, whether at work, at home or in the community, isn't because we're terrible people. It's because no one ever taught us how to talk through tough moments well.

We've been conditioned to believe silence is safer, confrontation is destructive, and that people just "can't handle the truth." So instead of speaking up with clarity and care, we avoid, explode or talk around the issue instead of through it.

Part I of this book is about why that happens—and the real costs to our workplaces, relationships, and communities.

This section lays the groundwork for everything that follows by pulling back the curtain on the *real* reason so many conversations go sideways. Spoiler alert: it's not the content, it's the approach.

What You'll Learn

In **Chapter 1: "We Need to Talk—But We Don't Know How,"** we dig into the social, cultural, and professional conditioning and the science that taught us to avoid hard conversations. You'll see how this learned behavior shows up everywhere—from friendships and marriages to office politics and high-stakes meetings. With relatable examples and one unforgettable cookout story (yes, it involves potato salad), you'll see how much miscommunication stems from fear, not failure.

We'll walk through real-life situations that start small: missed deadlines, unmet expectations, awkward silences but quickly spiral into resentment, confusion, and tension. You'll even meet a fictional tech company that almost lost everything not because of market forces, but because no one inside the company knew how to speak up, challenge decisions, or clarify confusion before it became a crisis.

We also talk about money, because make no mistake: ineffective communication doesn't just hurt feelings, it hits budgets. You'll learn how poor dialogue can lead to turnover, missed opportunities, lawsuits, and leadership breakdowns that cost millions.

In **Chapter 2: "What Is Conversational Competence?"**, we introduce a skill most people have never formally been taught but desperately need. Conversational competence is your ability to navigate high-stakes conversations with confidence, clarity, and emotional intelligence. We'll break it down, show you why it matters, and help you see the difference between people who talk *at* each other... and those who actually communicate.

You'll start by reflecting on the conversations you've been avoiding—because that's where your learning begins. You'll take an interactive conversational self-assessment (don't worry, it's insightful and a little funny), and uncover whether you're currently showing up as an Avoider, a Smooth Operator, a Verbal Warrior, or a full-on Conversationalist.

Then, we explore one of the most important truths in this entire book: most conflict isn't about the issue, it's about how the issue is discussed.

Using my husband's wisdom, "There's not so much doing right and wrong as there is understanding and misunderstanding," we'll unpack how timing, tone, location, and emotional energy all shape how a message lands. You'll see why the same words can spark peace or chaos, depending on where, when, and how they're delivered. Because saying "I have a loaded gun" lands *very* differently at a gun range than it does at a bank.

Through that lens, you'll learn why communication is never just about content; it's also about context.

Why This Matters

You can't improve what you haven't defined. Part I sets the stage for everything else in this book by helping you identify the communication patterns holding you back and how those patterns were formed in the first place.

We often walk into conversations hoping for the best, yet we are often completely unprepared. We assume we're being clear, even when we're being emotionally messy. We think we're being honest, even when we're being harsh. Or we think we're avoiding drama, when we're actually building a backlog of resentment that will eventually erupt.

Conversational competence isn't about avoiding conflict. It's about learning to move through it with skill.

And once you understand the *why* behind your avoidance, your missteps, or your default behaviors, you're finally in a position to change them. That's what this section gives you: awareness, language, and insight.

Before we introduce the DARE Model—a step-by-step framework for navigating tough conversations with clarity, confidence, and real results—in Part II, you'll understand the cost of not speaking up, the power of knowing how, and the urgency of building the skills you were never taught but now need in every area of your life.

Why Now?

We're in a world that is louder, faster, more reactive, and more polarized than ever. People are burning out, shutting down, lashing out—and too often, saying either nothing or saying too much with too little care.

If you're reading this, you're probably ready to show up differently. You don't want to win arguments—you want to be effective. You don't want to dominate conversations—you want to make them *matter*.

This is where that journey begins.

So take a deep breath, think about the conversations you've been dreading, and keep going. Because the clarity, confidence, and connection you've been hoping for all start with competence. And you're about to build it, one DARE step at a time.

Chapter 1

We Need to Talk, But We Don't Know How

Marissa stared at her phone, heart pounding, her thumb hovering uncertainly over the "send" button. The message had been drafted and re-drafted at least six times, each revision more carefully worded than the last. It was professional yet firm, clear yet respectful, a delicate dance of words designed to confront her coworker, Jonathan, about his consistently missed deadlines that were jeopardizing the success of their entire project.

Jonathan needs some guidance, but she hesitated because her mind raced with an avalanche of fears: Would this permanently damage their working relationship? Would Jonathan perceive her as aggressive, bossy, or overly critical? What if he took offense, became defensive, or worse, escalated the issue to their supervisor? After all, she wasn't even Jonathan's supervisor. She wasn't senior to him, and there was no official authority in her title that compelled him to listen.

Ultimately, Marissa sighed deeply, tapped "delete," and placed her phone facedown on her desk. Frustration surged through her chest as a familiar sense of resignation took hold. She knew the stakes were high; this project wasn't just another checkbox on her workload, it was a critical juncture. Successfully executed, it'd shine brightly on her résumé, potentially accelerating her promotion to the coveted senior management role she has long pursued. However, as things stood, with Jonathan underperforming, the project seemed destined for mediocrity, being slightly late, slightly over budget, and forgettable in every sense.

It wasn't supposed to be this way. The project had begun with so much promise, enthusiasm brimming in their initial meetings. Yet, when Marissa began to notice Jonathan's missed deadlines, sloppy work, and overpromising yet underdelivering, her dread of an awkward interaction kept her silent. Rather than addressing the root issue, she let the tension simmer quietly, unresolved and steadily poisoning the project and the air between them.

What Marissa experienced was far from unique. Every day, in boardrooms, break rooms, and bedrooms across the globe, vital conversations are avoided. We dodge discussions, postpone conflict, and suppress truth because we fear discomfort, confrontation, and relational fallout. It's a phenomenon deeply woven into the fabric of our personal and professional lives, sustained by deeply ingrained conditioning that we rarely stop to question or challenge.

But why do we behave this way? Why do intelligent, capable adults often feel so profoundly ill-equipped for essential conversations?

From our earliest days, we're carefully conditioned by culture, often subtly and unintentionally, to prioritize politeness over honesty, harmony over authenticity, and comfort over clarity. Parents hush children who ask uncomfortable questions loudly in grocery store aisles; teachers praise obedient quietness more frequently than inquisitive questioning. Even workplaces often discourage employees from raising uncomfortable perspectives or questions that may disrupt the status quo, even at the expense of productivity, collaboration, and innovation.

In short, we're taught to go with the flow, not ruffle feathers, and to "go along to get along."

Marissa had learned these lessons early. Growing up, she had watched her mother quietly endure disagreements with neighbors, smiling politely even as anger brewed inside. At school, outspoken peers were quickly labeled troublemakers and punished rather than listened to by teachers. At her first job, she'd seen managers subtly penalize coworkers who dared question authority figures or present fresh ideas that differed from their own. In every context, Marissa had absorbed one powerful message: confrontation equals conflict, and conflict is inherently negative.

This pervasive conditioning doesn't just harm personal growth; it actively impedes our ability to communicate effectively. The fear of conflict is so deeply embedded that it clouds our judgment, makes us question the legitimacy of our concerns, and ultimately silences our authentic voices. And what we misunderstand most profoundly is that difficult conversations aren't necessarily hostile or destructive. Confrontation, when handled skillfully, is one of the most powerful tools for clarity and positive change.

The consequences of avoiding these necessary interactions ripple outwards, infiltrating all aspects of our lives. Marissa's story is a professional, individual example, but these communication failures compound collectively, becoming systemic issues in marriages, families, organizations, and communities.

Consider marriages, where unresolved disagreements can fester and evolve into deep-seated resentments. Spouses stop discussing important issues, money, parenting styles, intimacy, and career decisions until they're drifting silently apart, unable to bridge the chasm that resentment creates. Therapists' offices are filled with couples who once loved deeply but who now struggle simply because they couldn't or wouldn't effectively communicate their needs and expectations.

Similarly, friendships dissolve under misunderstandings that might have been quickly cleared up had either friend dared to initiate the conversation. How often do we say, "It's not worth bringing up," until silence breeds distance, resentment, and eventual loss?

Workplaces are no different. Poor communication doesn't merely disrupt projects; the financial and reputational costs of these communication breakdowns can devastate entire companies. Avoiding tough conversations often leads to unclear roles, misunderstood goals, and unspoken grievances among team members. Employees who cannot or will not discuss conflicts openly grow frustrated, disengaged, and eventually leave. Productivity plummets, turnover rates climb, public scandals and lawsuits arise, and workplace culture deteriorates into a minefield of quiet quitters and subtle sabotage. A 2022 Gallup report revealed that poor communication and conflict avoidance cost U.S. businesses an estimated $359 billion annually, staggering losses that could largely be mitigated by simply learning to have better, clearer, and more impactful conversations.

The uncomfortable truth is this–poor and non-existent conversations don't only harm relationships, they harm everything: our productivity, emotional health, career advancement, and even the financial stability of the businesses we rely on. Avoidance quietly accumulates into a destructive force, eroding potential, profitability, trust, and the human connections we need most.

Thankfully, there's another path available, one we'll explore in depth throughout this book. This journey begins with acknowledging our fear, recognizing our conditioning, and consciously deciding to approach conversations differently. It demands that we begin to think of confrontation not as a battle to avoid, but as a necessary, sometimes uncomfortable, yet ultimately decisive step toward clarity, understanding, and effective expectation management.

Throughout this chapter, we'll unpack why we avoid tough conversations. We'll highlight compelling real-world scenarios across different contexts, including marriage disputes, workplace tensions, and the painfully polarized world of politics. We'll explore the significant business costs, underscoring how miscommunication and silence aren't merely emotional issues; they are concrete, measurable liabilities.

As we revisit Marissa's story throughout this chapter, you'll have opportunities to reconsider her approach and yours. Armed with new insight and practical tools, you'll be empowered to transform conversations from dreaded interactions into powerful tools for clarity, collaboration, and success.

Conditioning and Avoidance: How We Learned to Stay Silent

We intuitively know there's a cost to conversations we avoid, broken friendships, dysfunctional workplaces, divided communities, and stalled progress. But if we know avoidance is so damaging, why do we keep choosing it, again and again? To put it simply: it's not entirely our fault. Our tendency to dodge hard conversations didn't spring out of nowhere. It's deeply rooted in the cultural conditioning we've absorbed throughout our lives.

From childhood, we've been quietly trained to stay silent when things get uncomfortable. Consider this: as children, we quickly learned which questions made adults uneasy. "Why doesn't Uncle Greg live with Aunt Lisa anymore?" "Why does Grandma smell funny?" "How come Dad never talks to Grandpa?" Innocent questions like these were often met with sharp glances or swift whispers of, "We don't talk about that." The message was clear, even if unspoken: some topics are off-limits. And let's not even get started on the classic line: "Children are to be seen and not heard," "If you don't have anything nice to say don't say anything at all", "Don't Talk back", "Big boys don't cry/complain", "We don't talk about that outside the house", "Good girls don't talk like that." With these and other similar phrases, many of us were taught not just to keep quiet, but to avoid saying anything that might stir the pot. The lesson? Don't speak up, especially if what you're saying might cause a problem.

This conditioning only intensified as we grew older. In classrooms, teachers often praised students who stayed quiet and listened rather than those who spoke out or challenged ideas. Even when we were encouraged to "speak up," we quickly learned there were unspoken rules about what was acceptable and what was off-limits. Slowly, we absorbed a crucial lesson: being agreeable was rewarded; being confrontational, even constructively, was risky.

I vividly remember my version of this story. You can probably guess that I was not the "be seen and not heard" child. I think back to some of the things adults felt comfortable saying to me and calling me, because of my outspokenness.

One memory stands out. I was still a kid, and an adult said something that was just plain wrong. I spoke up, gladly, to correct them. I wasn't trying to be disrespectful; I honestly thought I was helping. But they didn't take it that way. The adult snapped at me with a tone so sharp it could've cut through concrete. My skin burned, not just from embarrassment, but from anger. I felt helpless, but I wasn't about to back down. I shot back with something wildly inappropriate for a child to say to an adult. And I got what was considered a "fitting punishment" for that era.

That moment did affect me, but not in the way the adults might have hoped. It didn't teach me to be quiet. It taught me to come out swinging. I stopped trying to soften my words or my message. I stopped considering how what I said might land. I figured, if I was going to get attacked for speaking up anyway, I might as well strike first and make it count.

But here's the part we don't talk about enough: I wasn't the only one who learned something that day.

I'll never forget what one of my cousins whispered later: "DeeDee, you say it, cause you're not scared." That moment stuck with me. While I learned to use my voice like a weapon, they learned to lock theirs away. My punishment didn't just shape how I handled conflict; it silenced others entirely.

Now, all these years later, I look at some of the people who witnessed that interaction. Many of them still haven't found their voices. When disagreement shows up, they shut down. Or they explode. That's it. No middle ground. No thoughtful pushback. Just silence or outrage, because none of us were taught how to navigate disagreement in a way that was honest, respectful, and effective.

What we all walked away with that day was a bit of dysfunction, just packaged differently. I learned to be blunt, sometimes too blunt. Others learned to disappear. However, none of us learned how to have a productive and impactful conversation when things got tough.

By adulthood, our learned silence becomes second nature. In workplaces, we're frequently reminded, implicitly and explicitly, that confrontation, disagreement, or open critique can damage our professional futures. We watch as colleagues who speak openly are subtly punished, passed over for promotions, labeled "difficult," or quietly sidelined. Over time, we internalize the belief that avoidance isn't a sign of weakness; it's a strategic approach. And it's a strategy we cling to even when it doesn't serve us.

Culturally, this silence isn't limited by borders. Across the globe, cultures establish rules around what is acceptable to discuss openly. In some cultures, speaking directly about money or family issues is taboo, for example. In others, openly disagreeing with authority figures is seen as disrespectful. Regardless of the culture, one thing remains consistent: we internalize rules about what can and cannot be openly discussed, and we carry that into every relationship, from romantic to professional. But here's the kicker: this cultural conditioning isn't static. It evolves with us, shifting as our roles and expectations change.

For instance, a woman raised in a family where conflict was avoided at all costs may eventually become a team leader, expected to give critical feedback and advocate for her team in high-stakes meetings. The same person who was taught "don't start trouble" may now be told to "speak truth to power." The dissonance between those messages often leads to hesitation or guilt when stepping into a more vocal role.

Similarly, men who grew up hearing "be strong, don't complain" may find themselves in emotionally complex leadership situations, like supporting a team after layoffs or addressing employee burnout. Yet because they were conditioned to equate emotional transparency with weakness, they struggle to show empathy or ask for help themselves, even when it's expected of modern leaders.

Even cultural norms around authority shift. A professional raised in a hierarchical culture may enter a more egalitarian workplace where questioning ideas, even from senior leaders, is encouraged. But if they were taught that disagreement equals disrespect, they may freeze in meetings, default to silence, or feel constant anxiety around performance reviews.

In each case, the rules we learned in childhood don't disappear. They evolve with us, often clashing with the roles we're asked to play and the voices we're trying to use.

At work, this can be even more subtle. Employees quickly learn to read the room, and many decide silence is the safest strategy. According to the Society for Human Resource Management (SHRM), nearly two-thirds of US workers have witnessed or experienced workplace misconduct, and many of them didn't report it. Why? The overwhelming reason wasn't lack of evidence; it was fear of retaliation or being labeled a troublemaker.

And here's the kicker: In many cases, there was no explicit threat. No one said "don't speak up". But people still kept quiet. That's the power of culture. It teaches you how to behave without anyone ever saying a word. You learn what's safe and what's not. Over time, silence starts to feel like self-preservation, even when it's self-sabotage.

So, what does this mean for you?

The cultural conditioning we've absorbed, whether at home, in school, or at work, is powerful, pervasive, and often unconscious. But awareness is powerful too. When you recognize your avoidance as a learned behavior rather than an inherent personality flaw, you gain incredible leverage. Suddenly, your silence isn't inevitable; it's just a habit, one that can be changed.

Remember those neural pathways we talked about earlier? Each time we default to silence, we reinforce the existing path. But each time we intentionally step into a meaningful conversation, even when it feels uncomfortable, we forge a new one. This process takes practice, courage, and persistence, but it's entirely within your reach.

Here's something you might find fascinating: According to neuroscientist Dr. Caroline Leaf, author of *Switch On Your Brain*, creating a new neural pathway takes roughly 63 days of intentional practice. That's just two months to shift how you approach difficult conversations significantly. Just two months to move from silence and discomfort toward confidence and clarity. Is your career, your relationships, and your community worth 63 days of courageous practice?

You don't have to be perfect. You won't be, at least not immediately. You might stumble through your first few conversations awkwardly. However, what matters is that each attempt makes the next one easier. Every small step away from silence and toward open dialogue reshapes your brain, creating pathways that eventually become second nature.

Let's Reflect

Before we go further, let's pause for another quick activity. Reflect honestly on these questions:

- Think of an early memory where you were discouraged from speaking up or openly disagreeing. What happened, and how did it affect your behavior afterward?

- Can you identify times in your current life, at work or at home, where your conditioned silence holds you back?

- What's one small step you can take today to practice speaking up even when you're tempted to remain silent?

Write your reflections down, and don't worry about having all the answers just yet. Simply becoming aware of your patterns is already a decisive step. Recognizing these conditioned behaviors puts you firmly back in control, positioning you to choose courage and clarity over silence and avoidance.

The Cost of Avoidance: How Silence Impacts Relationships, Workplaces, and Communities

We've seen Marissa struggle to speak openly about Jonathan's underperformance, illustrating a familiar pattern: avoiding pivotal conversations to maintain comfort, even at significant personal cost. Yet, Marissa's hesitation, and ours, is more than just an individual failing; it's a widespread cultural and professional phenomenon. This avoidance carries real consequences, measured in broken relationships, toxic workplaces, failed projects, and polarized communities.

Avoidance at Home: Relationships on the Brink

Let's start close to home. According to a 2022 study published in the *Journal of Social and Personal Relationships*, 68% of adults reported actively avoiding difficult conversations in their personal relationships, despite recognizing that such avoidance would ultimately increase conflict and stress.

Consider marriage: When partners sidestep conversations about finances, parenting differences, intimacy issues, or personal frustrations, the result is rarely positive. A Harvard psychology report recently revealed that couples who consistently avoid difficult conversations are significantly more likely to divorce within ten years compared to those who regularly communicate, even if that communication feels awkward or uncomfortable.

Take Jessica and Terrence, for instance, a seemingly happy couple married for eleven years, raising three kids together. On the surface, their marriage looked healthy. However, privately, Jessica felt burdened by financial pressures she never discussed. Terrence struggled with resentment about balancing household responsibilities. Neither spoke up; neither had the conversational competence. Over the years, quiet tension had become explosive arguments, until counseling seemed their only hope. Their marriage, now looking divorce in the eyes, faced uncertainty because difficult conversations seemed too uncomfortable at first, too complicated later, and eventually felt impossible.

The Price of Friendships: Losing Bonds Over Silence

It's not only romantic relationships that suffer. Friendships, too, falter when important truths remain unsaid. According to Pew Research, nearly 40% of Americans admitted to ending a friendship rather than facing an awkward conversation to resolve conflict or clarify misunderstandings.

This one hits home for me.

A few years ago, I had a very close friend, someone I deeply loved and considered family. Our friendship was real, layered, and full of history. Her children even called me "Momma D." But one day, something changed. I started noticing some things in her relationship that gave me pause. Not big dramatic events, just little patterns and comments that made me feel like something might be off. I didn't have facts. I didn't have proof. What I had was a gut feeling and a growing discomfort that I didn't know how to name.

I wanted to say something, but I didn't know *what* to say, or *how much*. I didn't want to seem judgmental or accusatory. I didn't want to cross a line or come off like I was inserting myself into something that wasn't mine to fix. Most of all, I didn't want to damage a friendship I cherished. So, I stayed silent.

I convinced myself I was being respectful, that it wasn't my place. That I should just pray, stay supportive, and keep showing up. But underneath that rationalization was fear: fear that she'd be hurt, angry, or feel betrayed by me bringing it up. And if I'm honest, I wasn't just afraid of losing the friendship, I was afraid I wouldn't be able to navigate the conversation *well enough* to avoid breaking something important between us.

Eventually, time revealed what I had suspected. And in the aftermath, she asked me a quiet, heartbreaking question: "Did you see anything? Did you know?"

And I had to answer her honestly. Yes, I had seen *something*. Not a single event. Not a smoking gun. But I had seen *enough* to know something felt off. Enough to wrestle with saying something, and choose silence instead.

Her hurt was precisely what I had tried to avoid, but I felt it anyway. I hadn't protected her, and I hadn't protected our friendship either. I had just delayed the damage.

That's the thing about silence: it feels like safety in the moment, but sometimes, it's just a slow leak in a relationship. A quiet erosion of trust. And by the time it's obvious, it can be too late.

Looking back, I realized it wasn't just fear that held me back; it was a lack of preparation. I didn't have the language, the strategy, or the tools to hold a conversation like that with clarity and care. I knew something needed to be said, but I didn't know how to say it without risking everything.

Today, I do have those tools. And having them makes a difference.

When you know how to approach challenging conversations with intention, skill, and emotional intelligence, it doesn't erase the risk, but it *does* increase your confidence. It gives you a roadmap when everything feels messy and uncertain. Now, when I show up for the people I care about, I don't just bring love, I bring language, strategy, and courage.

That's what this work is really about. Not just getting people to talk, but giving them the ability to do it well, even when it's hard, especially when it matters.

Workplace Consequences: *The Financial Impact of Unspoken Issues*

While the personal costs of avoiding tough conversations are painful enough, the professional consequences can be detrimental, especially for businesses. A recent McKinsey study revealed an astonishing figure: ineffective communication and conflict avoidance cost American companies roughly $359 billion per year in lost productivity, high employee turnover, and litigation expenses.

Turnover, specifically, becomes a hidden epidemic. Gallup's 2023 workplace survey reported that 75% of voluntary employee departures were directly linked to unresolved workplace issues or poor managerial communication. Employees don't typically leave their jobs; they leave uncomfortable or toxic situations where they feel powerless to be heard or to change.

Consider Simone, a talented graphic designer at a respected marketing firm. Simone's boss frequently assigned her last-minute work without notice, creating ongoing disruption, stress, and resentment. Rather than express her concerns, Simone remained quiet, believing confrontation would mark her as problematic, not a team player. Eventually, overwhelmed, overworked, and undervalued, she resigned without explanation. Her employer lost an excellent talent, one that could have been retained had Simone felt safe to communicate openly. The cost of replacing Simone was high and could have been avoided by simply teaching the team, including Simone and her boss, the skills of conversational competence.

Let's beware not to gloss over conversational competence as the problem of a few timid colleagues or the occasional domineering manager. The consequences of conversational avoidance become clearest when examining specific cases, such as the near-collapse of InnovaTech. A respected tech firm known for innovation and rapid growth, InnovaTech found itself suddenly hemorrhaging talent, revenue, and reputation.

At first glance, the cause seemed mysterious: there were no obvious external pressures or dramatic industry shifts. Internally, however, the truth was stark. Employees routinely avoided speaking honestly about critical project failures, client dissatisfaction, and managerial incompetence. Senior executives feared that admitting mistakes would appear weak, and frontline employees worried that a critique would jeopardize their promotions or jobs. Slowly, silence became the culture. Projects stalled, clients left dissatisfied, and talented employees left the company.

It wasn't until InnovaTech faced bankruptcy and commissioned external audits that the truth came to light. Auditors conducted a comprehensive review of internal emails, project close-out reports, employee exit interviews, and meeting records across departments. What they uncovered wasn't just operational inefficiency; it was a culture of silence.

Critical concerns raised by staff were never escalated to management. Project teams failed to communicate changes across departments, resulting in missed deadlines and duplicated efforts. Senior leaders made decisions in silos, without input from those closest to the issues at hand. Communication breakdowns weren't just present; they were systemic.

The audit revealed that these communication gaps were the underlying cause of the company's collapse, not market failure or flawed products. The silence was costing InnovaTech nearly $50 million annually in lost projects, high turnover, and operational misfires. Once the hard conversations finally started, although uncomfortable, the company began its slow recovery.

Scandal, Lawsuits, and Bad Press: Potential Costs of Silence

On a broader level, silence can have direct legal and financial repercussions. A SHRM survey found that approximately **48% of U.S. employees** had witnessed workplace misconduct but said nothing, primarily due to fears of retaliation or negative labeling. Such unaddressed misconduct often escalates, ultimately exploding into public scandals, lawsuits, or substantial financial penalties.

One of the most notable examples is the 2016 financial scandal involving Wells Fargo. Investigations revealed a deeply ingrained culture in which employees feared speaking out about unethical sales practices. Instead of openly addressing issues, silence reigned. Ultimately, these conversations — the ones people didn't know how to have — cost the bank over $3 billion in fines, settlements, and reputational damage, vividly illustrating the steep price companies pay when they fail to build a culture rooted in conversational competence, honesty, and transparency.

Polarized Communities: Silence Fuels Division

Currently, our cultural climate is strained to the breaking point. We're increasingly divided, not simply by differing beliefs, but by an unwillingness to speak honestly and openly about those differences. Our collective inability to have meaningful conversations on topics where we disagree isn't just uncomfortable; it actively holds back progress, stifles growth, and leaves our most vulnerable populations hanging in the balance.

Consider the conversations we tend to avoid most: those surrounding poverty, education, healthcare, immigration, race, and social justice. These topics spark powerful emotions and strong opinions, so we often choose silence, convincing ourselves it's easier than confrontation. But here's the hard truth: these very conversations, where we most fiercely disagree, are precisely the dialogues we need most urgently. Our silence here doesn't maintain peace; it delays solutions.

When we avoid talking openly about poverty because it's uncomfortable, we also delay strategies that could feed the hungry or house the homeless. When education becomes too divisive to discuss openly, we allow countless children to fall further behind academically, thereby robbing them of future opportunities. And when topics like race or equity feel too charged to address, the most vulnerable members of our communities remain at risk, stuck in cycles of systemic inequity because genuine dialogue never takes place.

This isn't theoretical. It's happening right now, in our neighborhoods, schools, and workplaces. The Pew Research Center revealed a startling statistic: **85% of Americans** feel political discourse has become so hostile that they actively avoid conversations with neighbors, coworkers, and even family members who hold opposing views. Instead of talking, listening, and understanding one another, we're building walls of silence, retreating into comfortable echo chambers where our biases grow louder and empathy quietly fades away.

Think about the last family gathering, community event, or workplace networking event you attended. How many topics felt instantly off-limits, quietly avoided because someone might get upset? How many meaningful conversations were shut down, leaving unresolved misunderstandings and tensions simmering beneath polite smiles and casual conversations about the weather or sports?

We justify avoidance as self-protection. But the cost of this protective silence is devastatingly high. When we stop communicating across our differences, we stop truly connecting. Real, sustainable progress in our neighborhoods, schools, businesses, and political systems requires conversation. It demands facing the discomfort and stepping willingly into dialogue with those whose perspectives challenge our own.

History repeatedly proves this point: every significant advancement, whether in human rights, economic justice, public health, or education, began with difficult, often heated, but ultimately productive conversations. Change comes when we lean into discomfort, not away from it.

Avoiding tough conversations is more than just a personal failing; it's a collective crisis. The stakes are real: children, education, families, industry, a country, and our shared future depend on bridging divides rather than widening them.

Avoidance keeps us stuck exactly where we are, perpetually circling problems instead of solving them. But what if we learned to embrace these disagreements? What if we developed the skill to hold critical conversations respectfully, clearly, and intentionally?

That's precisely why conversational competence is so important, not only for our individual lives but for the world around us. The conversations we aren't having right now are precisely the ones that matter most. To create lasting change, we must first choose to speak, and do so in ways that are efficient, effective, and productive. It's not about talking just to say something; it's about speaking because we genuinely have something valuable to contribute.

Time to Talk: A Cultural Shift

Avoidance isn't safe; it's incredibly risky. Silence doesn't protect relationships or businesses; it damages them profoundly. This recognition requires a radical shift in how we approach difficult conversations.

Here's the great news: **you're not stuck this way forever.**

Avoiding tough conversations isn't some hardwired personality trait you're doomed to carry for life. Think of it like this, remember when you were a kid, and you had shortcuts to get everywhere? Maybe it was a path through the woods or a trail across a grassy field. You took those shortcuts so often that you wore down the grass and carved out a path without even thinking about it.

Then one day, you got a bike. And suddenly, that old path didn't make sense anymore. You found a new route — one that was smoother, more efficient, and made better use of your new tool. No one had to tell you to stop using the old path. You didn't feel guilty about the worn grass. You just had a better way to get where you were going.

Your brain works the same way.

It's full of little pathways, neural connections, that act just like those shortcuts through your neighborhood. The more you use one, the smoother and easier it becomes.

Avoidance? Cultural conditioning away from speaking up or risking confrontation or conflict? Those are just a well-worn trail you've walked for years, probably without even realizing it.

But now, you've got a new tool. And with it, a better way forward.

Now, trying to erase that trail (or "unlearn" avoidance and cultural conditioning) can feel like attempting to replant every blade of grass you flattened over decades — pretty exhausting, right? Thankfully, there's a simpler, smarter way: just start riding your bike, driving your car, being chauffeured, taking a different path. Instead of forcing yourself to "stop avoiding," you intentionally create new, healthier trails by choosing courage, clarity, empathy, and productive conversations again and again.

Each time you speak up when your heart says, "Stay quiet," you're actively forging new paths in your brain, forming fresh neural connections that slowly become your new normal. Eventually, these conversations won't feel so intimidating or awkward; they'll just feel like what you naturally do.

And the payoff? It's huge. Learning how to handle impactful conversations effectively doesn't just lower your stress level (though, believe me, it does!). It improves your relationships, boosts workplace productivity, and helps build communities that communicate, understand, and grow together.

Remember: this isn't just self-reflection — it's the start of a fundamental shift. Identifying these patterns now enables you to replace avoidance with intentional action as we continue to explore how to transform these conversations from dreaded moments into catalysts for meaningful change.

In the next sections, using the DARE Model, we'll explore concrete tools and strategies, practical, realistic steps, that make having meaningful conversations feel less daunting, less overwhelming, and far more achievable. You don't need to erase decades of cultural conditioning overnight; you simply need the courage and curiosity to start practicing.

The next conversation you have might feel awkward at first, but remember, that's okay. Awkwardness means you're growing, changing, and actively reshaping your communication skills and neural pathways.

The best part? You won't have to navigate this alone.

That's where the D.A.R.E. Model comes in.

It's the framework we'll use throughout this book to move from silence and survival mode to clarity, confidence, and connection. D.A.R.E. gives you a step-by-step process to approach difficult conversations with emotional intelligence and strategy—not just instinct or impulse.

You'll learn how to describe the issue without escalating it, acknowledge realities without minimizing differences, review the narratives running the show in your head, and engage in a way that invites dialogue instead of division.

This model won't erase discomfort, but it will give you something to hold onto when the conversation gets hard.

By the end of this book, you'll be armed with the insights, tools, and confidence to approach even the most challenging conversations as opportunities, not threats.

Chapter 1 Recap: Why We Suck at Talking to Each Other

Cliff Notes, Dethra-Style

Let's be honest: we're not inherently bad people; we've just been taught some bad habits when it comes to communication. This chapter peeled back the layers on **why** we avoid the conversations that matter most and what it's costing us when we do.

Key Takeaways:

- **Avoidance is everywhere**, in marriages, workplaces, friendships, and community spaces. We dodge hard conversations because we're afraid of discomfort, rejection, or fallout.

- **Our silence is not neutral.** It costs us. Personally and professionally. We miss out on opportunities, damage relationships, slow progress, and, if you're a business, hemorrhage money.

- **Conditioning runs deep.** From childhood, we're told "don't stir the pot," "stay in your place," or the classic "kids should be seen, not heard." Over time, that messaging trains us to stay silent, especially when the thing that *needs* to be said is tough to say or may be met with opposition.

- **The result? Dysfunction.** Some of us learned to lash out. Others learned to disappear. Either way, we weren't taught **how** to navigate disagreement, conflict, or hard truths with clarity and compassion.

- **Neuroscience is the cheat code.** Avoidance is a neural pathway, your brain's go-to shortcut. But here's the empowering part: you don't have to "unlearn" everything. You just need to start building new, better paths. With practice, new becomes natural.

- **Culture shapes communication.** At work, people often stay quiet, not because they want to, but because they're afraid. SHRM data shows fear of retaliation is a real barrier. And when people don't feel safe to speak, things go unsaid until everything falls apart. This silence is expensive.

- **Our communities suffer, too.** When we avoid conversations around politics, race, equity, education, and justice, progress stalls. These are the exact conversations that move society forward, but fear keeps us quiet. And silence keeps us stuck.

Why This Matters:

You can't change what you won't confront. And you can't confront what you won't talk about.

Conversational competence isn't just a feel-good concept; it's a necessary skill for building stronger relationships, leading with integrity, and driving real change in every space you occupy.

This chapter laid the groundwork. We've named the problem, unpacked its origins, and exposed the cost of remaining silent.

Now that we know what's broken, it's time to learn how to fix it.

Let's go.

Chapter 2

What Is Conversational Competence?

Let me tell you about the time I almost started a full-blown family feud… over potato salad.

It was a summer cookout, hot and humid, full of folks who brought dishes wrapped in foil and opinions wrapped in shade. You know the type of event. One aunt was wearing church heels on grass, another uncle was holding court under the pecan tree, we were all laughing at my cousin who swore he was the best-dressed person there despite wearing a plaid short set that had him looking like a picnic table cloth, and the kids were running wild, until someone threatened their lives for getting too close to the food table. You know, the chaotic family gatherings we all live for.

Now, I wasn't looking for trouble. I was just trying to fix a plate. But as I scanned the spread, I saw two bowls of potato salad that, by appearance, were not made by the same person, and made the rookie mistake of asking, loud enough for the wrong aunt to hear, *"Who made this one?"*

You would've thought I slapped somebody's child.

Gasps. Side-eyes. A whole conversation broke out *about* me, but not *with* me. And the one person brave enough to say anything didn't actually start a conversation with me. They just said loudly to the air, *"So, what is she trying to say?"*

And here's the kicker: I wasn't trying to say anything shady. I just wanted to know which one was made by my favorite aunt, the one who makes potato salad exactly the way I like it.

That's when it hit me. The problem wasn't *what* I said; it was *how* it landed. And the bigger problem? No one wanted to talk about it directly. We danced around it, made jokes, pretended to be unbothered when feelings were clearly hurt, and avoided each other by the dessert table. Weeks later, people were still mad, and no one could even remember exactly what I said. But they sure remembered how they felt.

That, my friend, is why this chapter matters.

Because most of the time, conflict isn't about the thing we're arguing over, it's about the way we handle the conversation around it. It's not the potato salad. It's the tone, the timing, the side-eyes, the assumptions, and the missing skill set that make it all worse.

In this chapter, we're going to clarify what **conversational competence** is, because it's more than just "talking well." It's about navigating tough, tense, or awkward moments with clarity, courage, and a sense of connection. We'll also take a quick quiz to see how well you're really doing (no judgment, just insight), and I'll delve into my go-to framework for getting it right: the **D.A.R.E. Model**.

By the time we're done here, you'll not only know what conversational competence looks like, but you'll also start building the skills to walk into the next disagreement with more grace, less drama, and fewer casualties. And, most importantly, you'll be able to ask about the potato salad without being written out of the will.

Defining Conversational Competence and Why It Matters

Is there a conversation you know you need to have with someone, but you've been holding off?

Be honest. Who came to mind just now?

Maybe it's with a coworker who keeps crossing boundaries. Or your partner, who hasn't noticed how disconnected things have become. Or your boss, who keeps overloading you while ignoring your contributions. You've played the conversation in your head a dozen times. You've rewritten the script and rehearsed it in the mirror. You've even imagined what they'll say in return.

But still… silence: no conversation in real life.

Now ask yourself: Why? Why haven't you had the conversation yet?

Maybe you've convinced yourself the timing isn't right. Or maybe you're hoping things will just "work themselves out." Maybe you're telling yourself it's not that serious. What's got your stomach in knots every time you think about bringing it up? Why?

If we're being real, the most common reason, the one people are rarely willing to say out loud, is this:

You're not sure you have the skills to handle the conversation in a way that won't cause a blow-up or damage the relationship.

It's not that you don't *want* to have the conversation. You just don't feel confident that you'll do it well. You suspect it might be a tough conversation, and deep down, you're worried that once it starts, it might spiral into misunderstanding, offense, tears, yelling, or long-term tension. And you're not wrong for feeling that way. Most of us were never taught how to navigate those moments with strategy, compassion, and clarity. So, we sit on our truth because we lack the confidence to bring it to light, and hope our silence will protect us.

But if you really sit with it, if you are daringly honest, you know your fear and silence are costing you. That's why **conversational competence** matters.

Because the truth is: avoiding the conversation won't make it go away. It just makes the consequences louder later.

So what is Conversational Competence?

Let's break it down. Conversational competence is the ability to have meaningful, productive, and emotionally intelligent conversations, especially when the stakes are high, emotions are involved, and disagreement is likely.

It's not just about "talking well." It's about navigating dialogue with purpose, presence, and people in mind. It's about knowing:

When to speak

What to say

How to say it

And how to stay engaged when things get uncomfortable

It's about being able to express yourself clearly without crushing someone else in the process.

It's being able to listen without losing yourself. It's being able to disagree without devaluing the other person. It's being able to stay grounded when emotions are rising.

And here's the part most people miss: It's a skill. Which means it can be learned, practiced, and improved, just like writing, managing money, or learning to drive.

You don't have to be naturally "good at confrontation" or an extrovert. Conversational competence is for everyone, introverts, overthinkers, hot-heads, harmonizers, and even those of us who need a pep talk just to send a text that says, "Hey, can we talk?"

The Real-World Payoff: Why It Matters (More Than Ever)

We live in a world where the ability to communicate with people we disagree with is no longer optional–it's essential.

Whether you're trying to lead a team, protect a relationship, advocate for yourself, or drive change in your community, your ability to hold meaning-ful conversations is the bridge between idea and impact.

Let's take it out of the abstract for a second.

Imagine these situations:

- A colleague is taking credit for your work. You're angry, feel resent-ful, and feel overlooked. Not to mention, there are material conse-quences of putting your promotion or raise in jeopardy. But you remain silent because of fear of retaliation.

- A friend is consistently an hour or more late for scheduled events, and you feel they do not respect your time. You don't want to seem needy, but the imbalance is eating at you.

- A family member made a hurtful comment at dinner. You know they didn't "mean it like that," but letting it slide doesn't sit right with you. A rift forms in the relationship as you begin to pull away, or worse, as you unintentionally stir up discord by complaining about the situation to other family members.

In each case, something needs to be said. But most people won't say it. Not because it doesn't matter, but because they don't know *how*.

That hesitation, that gap between what we feel and what we're willing to say, is where relationships fracture, resentment builds, and progress stalls.

Conversational competence closes that gap.

The ability to communicate effectively in tough moments isn't just a "nice to have"; it's a professional and personal power move.

In the workplace, it shows up as:

- Confidently advocating for yourself in a performance review

- Navigating conflict without blowing up a team dynamic

- Giving and receiving feedback in a way that builds trust, not tension

In personal life, it shows up as:

- Setting boundaries without guilt

- Resolving tension without shutting down or lashing out

- Deepening your relationships through honesty and active listening

And in your community, it shows up as:

- Engaging in conversations across differences

- Listening to perspectives that challenge you without feeling personally attacked

- Being the kind of leader who invites dialogue, not just compliance

The return on conversational competence is massive. It builds trust, increases influence, strengthens connections, and reduces the stress of holding everything in.

What It's Not

Let's be clear, conversational competence is not about being "nice." It's not about always agreeing. It's not about tiptoeing, sugarcoating, or making everyone feel good at the expense of progress.

Conversational competence is not weak. It's not passive. And it's not performative.

It's honest. Intentional. Bold. It's learning to say what needs to be said, in a way that others can hear and respond to, even when it's hard.

It doesn't mean the conversation will be easy. It doesn't guarantee you won't still walk away with a knot in your stomach. But it *does* mean you'll walk away knowing you showed up with clarity, not chaos.

You Don't Have to Be Perfect, Just Prepared

You don't need to get it 100% right every time. You just need to start practicing.

The people who are great at this aren't fearless. They're not immune to nerves or doubt. They've just trained the muscle. They've done the work to understand their style and cultural conditioning. They've stopped avoiding and started leaning in, with tools, intention, and confidence.

And the best part? You can too.

So, here's your invitation:

Think about that conversation you've been avoiding. The one that popped into your head earlier. Don't bury it again. Don't put it back on the shelf. Keep it in your pocket as we go.

Because you're going to get the tools you need to approach it with competence, confidence, and care.

Reflection Prompt

Write this down or share it with a friend:

"The conversation I've been avoiding is _____. I haven't had it because _____. But I'm ready to learn how."

There Has to Be a Better Way to Talk

Let's be honest. Most of us weren't taught how to have honest, respectful, productive conversations when emotions are high or opinions are divided. We were taught how to speak well in interviews, how to send professional emails, how to give a great presentation, but not how to look someone in the eye and say:

- That hurt me.

- I don't agree with you, but I still want to understand.

- This dynamic isn't working, and we need to talk about it.

We were told to be kind, but not how to speak truthfully without causing harm.

We were told to "not take things personally," but not how to separate fact from feeling.

We were told to pick our battles, but never taught how to endure them without losing the relationship.

So when conflict arises, or tension builds, we either avoid it, bulldoze through it, sugarcoat it, or silently stew in it. And let's be clear: none of those approaches actually help. They just delay or disguise the damage.

But here's the good news: there is a better way to talk.

And more importantly, a better way to listen, engage, and lead when conversations get hard.

The Model: D.A.R.E.

That model is called **D.A.R.E.**

D.A.R.E. is a simple yet powerful framework that helps you navigate high-stakes conversations with courage, strategy, and emotional intelligence. I created it because I needed something that worked in real-life conversations, not just ideal scenarios in training manuals. Something that worked in the middle of a tense meeting, a difficult family dinner, or a late-night heart-to-heart. Something that made space for both truth and tact. Honesty and healing. Boundaries and bridges. It has helped thousands of people like you stay grounded when emotions are rising and chart a path forward when silence or shouting feel like the only two options.

Here's what it stands for:

- **Describe vs. Interpret** – Start with the facts, not your interpretation or assumptions.

- **Acknowledge similarities without minimizing differences** – Recognize where you and the other person agree without ignoring the areas where there is disagreement.

- **Review the narratives you have accepted as fact** – Examine the story or narrative shaping the conflict or misunderstanding.

- **Engage for conversation, not conversion** – Invite meaningful dialogue that opens the door for collaboration or resolution.

You don't need to use all four steps perfectly every time. However, understanding how these pieces work together provides a roadmap for conversations that matter, without leaving you feeling lost or reactive.

Case Study: A Promotion Saved by a Conversation

Jordan was a strong performer, and everyone was aware of it. So when a less experienced colleague was promoted to a role Jordan had diligently been working toward, it felt like a gut punch. Instead of lashing out or shutting down, Jordan decided to take a different approach. He sent his manager a quick ping on Teams to grab a spot on their calendar: "I see you have a 20-minute opening on Tuesday. I'd like to stop by to discuss my latest project.

He D.A.R.E.D to have the conversation.

- **Describe: Start with the facts, not your interpretation or assumptions.**

   Jordan didn't start with feelings or assumptions. He started with facts: "I've been here for five years. In that time, I've received 'exceeds expectations' on every performance evaluation, never submitted a late project, and consistently received 5-star ratings from my clients. Yet, I've watched people with lower performance scores and customer satisfaction ratings be promoted, some more than once."

- **Acknowledge: Recognize where you and the other person agree without ignoring the areas where there is disagreement.**

   He acknowledged the complexity and didn't assume ill intent: "I know you've consistently spoken highly of my work, and I truly value that recognition. I think we both agree that I've delivered at a

56

high level. At the same time, I'm noticing a gap between that shared recognition and the opportunities I've received for advancement, and that's what I want to discuss."

- **Review: Examine the story or narrative shaping the conflict or misunderstanding**

  Jordan gently surfaced the unspoken narrative: "There's a perception, one I've admittedly started to believe, that promotions here aren't always based on performance, but on relationships. And I want to be honest about how that belief is affecting my motivation to keep performing at the highest level and trust in the promotion process."

- **Engage: Invite meaningful dialogue that opens the door for collaboration or resolution.**

  And then, he invited the manager into a real dialogue: "I'm not here just to vent, I want to grow. If there's something I'm missing or something I need to do differently, I'm open to that. But I also want to understand what it really takes to move forward here, and how we can create more alignment between performance and opportunity."

That conversation? It didn't just clear the air; it opened a door.

Because Jordan's boss didn't feel attacked or put on the defensive, the conversation stayed productive. Instead of shutting down or explaining away their decisions, the manager leaned in, offering insight and context that Jordan had been missing. That openness made all the difference.

Jordan walked away with clarity, a development plan, and eventually, the promotion he wanted and the pay he deserved.

Because he didn't just confront the issue, he communicated through it.

That's what conversational competence looks like in motion. That's the power of D.A.R.E.

Why D.A.R.E. Works

It works because it's built on truth, not tricks. The D.A.R.E. model wasn't created in a lab. It was born in real rooms with real people and real problems.

Initially, it was something I quietly used to enhance my own conversational competence.

If you haven't guessed by now, I was not the "hide from the problem" type. I wasn't the avoider,I was the bulldozer. Bold. Direct. Comfortable in confrontation. I could get my way by outtalking, outmaneuvering, and outlasting just about anyone in a conversation.

But here's the thing: winning the moment often meant losing the relationship.

It wasn't until I shifted my focus from winning to connecting that everything changed. I started to value the relationship more than the result. And that's when I realized how much more I was actually getting: more trust, more clarity, more meaningful outcomes.

Once I had mastered the skill, I began to integrate it into my coaching sessions.

My clients were dealing with everything from work stress to broken trust, team dysfunction, family tension, you name it. They weren't looking for buzzwords or theories. They just wanted help saying what they needed to say in a way that would actually be heard, not just spoken.

- So I started noticing the conversations that worked.

- The ones that left people feeling heard, rather than hurt.

- The ones that moved things forward instead of just rehashing the past.

- The ones that created resolutions, even if an agreement wasn't possible.

- They all followed a similar rhythm. Not a script, but a structure.

That's what became the D.A.R.E. model. And once I saw the pattern, I started teaching it to leadership teams, entire departments, and eventually leading organizations.

And then, I stood on a TEDx stage and shared it with the world.

My talk, "Deeper Conversations About Taboo Topics at Work," has since reached over 100,000 people and opened doors for delivering workshops, trainings, and keynotes at Fortune 500 companies, government agencies, nonprofits, schools, universities, and faith-based organizations across the United States and globally.

But what means more to me than any stage or spotlight are the emails and LinkedIn DMs I get afterward.

- A woman who hadn't spoken to her mother in six years said she used D.A.R.E. to reach out, and they're now rebuilding.

- A manager who used D.A.R.E. to address poor team performance and connect more authentically and productively with her team. Now they lead the highest-producing team at the company.

- A high school student who said D.A.R.E. helped her finally ask her dad a question she was afraid to voice for years.

This model is effective because it offers a practical framework for developing genuine conversational competence. Not vague inspiration. Not a personality change. Just clear tools you can use, whether you're leading a team, navigating a tough relationship, or advocating for yourself.

D.A.R.E. doesn't teach you how to "win" a conversation. It teaches you how to show up with integrity, clarity, and care. It's about safeguarding the conversation itself, preserving the relationship beyond the moment, and ensuring outcomes that support long-term stability and performance. It's about learning how to stand firm and still leave space for others.

What sets D.A.R.E. apart?

- It's **simple**: Four steps you can remember, even when emotions are high. Describe. Acknowledge. Review. Engage.

- It's **practical**: You can use it at work, at home, with clients, with loved ones, or even with yourself.

- It's **scalable**: It works for one-on-one conversations, team dynamics, or large-scale community dialogue and culture shifts.

- And it's **human**: It leaves space for grace, vulnerability, and growth.

I've polled my participants since using the D.A.R.E. Model, and **92%** of participants reported that the model helped them express something they had previously been afraid to say. Additionally, **78%** of participants said they resolved a personal or professional conflict within 30 days using the model, and **45%** reported stronger team collaboration. D.A.R.E. is giving people their voice back. It's helping leaders lead better. It's helping families heal. It's helping people say, "We need to talk", and actually know what to say next.

It works because it's built on truth, not tricks.

D.A.R.E.

Your Turn: Call to Action

Conversational Competence Assessment

As you continue through this book, I'm going to break the D.A.R.E. Model down, one chapter at a time. You'll get real-life examples, guided practice, and a clear roadmap to use this framework in your own life.

You don't have to master it all at once. You don't even have to be good at it yet.

You just have to start.

Because the conversation you've been avoiding? The one that keeps you up at night? The one that could shift everything if it goes well?

You're going to be ready for it.

Let's take this one step at a time, beginning with assessing how well you really handle hard conversations– your conversational competence.

No judgment. No shame. Just insight.

Instructions:

This isn't about your personality; it's about your current skill level when it comes to navigating conversations that carry weight. Not small talk. Not office chit-chat.

We're talking about the moments when your stomach tightens, your voice shakes, or your instincts tell you to run.

Answer honestly, not how you want to respond, but how you typically respond right now. This assessment is about awareness, not perfection. Once you know where you are, you can start leveling up.

1. **When a conversation gets tense, I...**

    A. Get quiet and try to make it end quickly.

    B. Smooth it over with humor or a quick subject change.

    C. Tackle it directly, even if it gets heated.

    D. Stay grounded and focus on understanding and being understood.

2. **I believe conflict is...**

    A. Something to avoid whenever possible.

    B. Uncomfortable, but part of life.

    C. A battle to be won.

    D. A necessary doorway to growth.

3. **If I need to address a sensitive issue, I usually...**

    A. Keep it to myself and hope it passes.

    B. Drop hints and hope the person gets it.

    C. Say it all at once, no filter.

    D. Prepare what to say and choose my timing carefully.

4. **When I hear something I strongly disagree with, I...**

    A. Say nothing and walk away.

    B. Try to nudge the conversation in another direction.

    C. Jump in and argue my point.

    D. Ask thoughtful questions and share my view calmly.

5. **When someone gives me critical feedback, I...**

    A. Feel defeated and replay it in my head for days.

    B. Smile and say "thanks" even if I disagree.

    C. Push back right away and explain myself.

    D. Take it in, reflect, and decide what's useful.

6. People often describe me as...

A. Easygoing, quiet, or reserved.

B. Friendly, diplomatic, or non-confrontational.

C. Bold, direct, or opinionated.

D. Thoughtful, honest, and clear.

7. After a difficult conversation, I usually feel...

A. Drained or full of regret.

B. Relieved it's over, even if nothing got solved.

C. Glad I got it off my chest.

D. Satisfied and clearer, even if it wasn't easy.

8. In group settings, when disagreement arises, I...

A. Stay silent and wait for it to pass.

B. Try to play peacemaker and keep things light.

C. Step in to defend my point of view.

D. Stay engaged and help move the conversation forward.

9. I struggle the most with...

A. Starting the conversation at all.

B. Saying how I really feel without sugarcoating.

C. Staying calm when I feel disrespected.

D. Nothing specific, I've practiced and grown in this area.

10. When a friend or colleague offends me, I...

A. Don't say anything, I just distance myself.

B. Drop passive-aggressive hints or make jokes about it.

C. Call it out right then and there.

D. Address it directly but respectfully.

11. I avoid tough conversations because…

A. I don't want to be misunderstood or hurt someone.

B. I'm afraid of making things worse.

C. I assume they'll get defensive and it'll escalate.

D. I don't,I lean in when it matters.

12. If someone's tone feels aggressive or condescending, I…

A. Freeze or shut down.

B. Smile and try to steer it back to neutral.

C. Match their energy, don't come for me unless I send for you.

D. Acknowledge the tone and keep the conversation productive.

13. I see disagreement as…

A. Stressful.

B. A sign we should change the subject.

C. A challenge I'm always ready for.

D. A natural part of growth and learning.

14. When I've said something wrong, I…

A. Avoid the person and hope they forget.

B. Apologize lightly, then move on fast.

C. Defend my intentions.

D. Own it, apologize sincerely, and try to do better.

15. In conversations that matter, my goal is to…

A. Avoid tension.

B. Keep everyone comfortable.

C. Make sure I'm heard loud and clear.

D. Create clarity, connection, and resolution.

Your Results

How to Score Your Results

At the end of the quiz, count how many times you selected each letter:

- **A** = Avoider _____
- **B** = Smooth Operator _____
- **C** = Verbal Warrior _____
- **D** = Conversationalist _____

The letter you chose most often reveals your current level of conversational competence.

If you're tied between two letters, read both descriptions; chances are you're transitioning between levels, and that's a powerful place to grow from.

This isn't about judgment, it's about awareness. Now that you know where you are, you can learn how to level up.

A's: *The Avoider*

You're like: T'Challa (*Black Panther,* early leadership moments)

You value harmony and keeping the peace, but sometimes, that means holding your truth hostage. Like T'Challa before he fully embraced the weight of his role, you wrestle with when to speak and when to remain silent. The fear of confrontation is real, but your voice matters, and learning to use it skillfully will elevate everything around you.

B's: *The Smooth Operator*

You're like: Charlotte York (*Sex and the City*)

Gracious, composed, and masterful at reading the room, you're the peacemaker. But like Charlotte, you sometimes avoid the messy middle. You'd rather charm your way around discomfort than dive into it. You don't need to lose your kindness, just add courage. Because sugarcoating helps no one when the truth is what's needed.

C's: The Verbal Warrior

You're like: Miranda Priestly (*The Devil Wears Prada*) meets Spock (*Star Trek*) on a bad day

You don't avoid hard conversations; you dominate them. You've got the facts, the strategy, and the delivery... but sometimes forget the human on the other end. Like Miranda, your sharpness gets results, but at what relational cost? And like Spock, logic rules, but emotion matters too. Add empathy to your arsenal, and your impact will multiply.

D's: The Conversationalist

You're like: Maxine Shaw (*Living Single*) meets Atticus Finch (*To Kill a Mockingbird*)

You strike a balance between truth and tact, and conviction and care. Like Maxine, you're quick-witted and fearless, and like Atticus, you aim to understand before being understood. You don't shy away from the uncomfortable, and you've got the rare ability to hold space for both honesty and healing. Keep honing that gift, it's leadership in motion.

Chapter 2 Recap: What Is Conversational Competence?

Cliff Notes, Dethra-Style

This chapter began with a cookout, some side-eyes, and a nearly tragic case of potato salad politics, but it was never really about the food. It was about how easily conversations can go off track when we don't have the skills to keep them on the right path. You learned that **conversational competence** isn't about being smooth or sounding smart. It's about having the courage, clarity, and emotional intelligence to navigate high-stakes, high-emotion conversations without blowing things up or backing away entirely.

We got honest about the conversations you've been avoiding, took a self-assessment to find out how you really show up in those moments, and busted the myth that good communication is something you're either born with or not. Spoiler: It's a skill. And yes, you can learn it.

You also got your first look at the D.A.R.E. model, a framework designed for real-life conversations, not just the hypothetical ones people practice in training and then forget when tension arises. D.A.R.E. is your tool to show up, speak up, and still keep the relationship intact.

Key Takeaways:

- **Conversational competence** is the ability to hold meaningful, emotionally intelligent dialogue when it matters most.

- Avoiding tough conversations doesn't solve the problem; it just delays the fallout.

- You don't need to be fearless or extroverted. You need a plan and a practiced skill set.

- The D.A.R.E. model provides four steps: **Describe, Acknowledge, Review, and Engage**, which serve as tools to guide real conversations in real life.

- This isn't about "winning" conversations. It's about showing up with clarity and care, and walking away with trust, understanding, and forward movement.

Why This Matters:

The conversations we avoid are often the ones that matter most.

Whether it's a misunderstanding at work, a relationship feeling out of sync, or a personal truth you've been holding in, learning to communicate through it, not around it, is what builds trust, deepens connection, and moves things forward.

We weren't taught how to do this when we were growing up. But now? You're learning. And it's a game-changer.

Part II

Executive Summary: The D.A.R.E. Model

Most of us were never formally taught how to have the conversations that really matter. We learned how to write a résumé, give a presentation, and maybe even manage a project. But how to speak up when things get uncomfortable? How to address tension in a way that doesn't make everything worse? How to be clear without being cruel?

That's a different skill set altogether. One that most people don't even realize they're missing until a moment of misunderstanding costs them trust, opportunity, or peace of mind.

That's where the **D.A.R.E. Model** comes in.

This isn't a theory. It's not a set of fluffy communication tips. The D.A.R.E. Model is a practical, proven framework that teaches you how to navigate high-stakes conversations with clarity, confidence, and emotional intelligence.

It's built for people who:

- Lead teams but struggle to manage conflict

- Want to advocate for themselves without blowing up the relationship

- Are you tired of walking on eggshells or bulldozing through people. Know they need to have *the conversation,* but don't know where to start

Whether you're an executive, an emerging leader, a parent, a partner, or a person trying to do better in difficult moments, this model is for you.

So what is D.A.R.E.?

D.A.R.E. stands for:

- **Describe vs Interpret** – Start with the facts, not your interpretation or assumptions.

- **Acknowledge similarities without minimizing differences** – Recognize where you and the other person agree without ignoring where you differ.

- **Review the narrative you have accepted as fact** – Surface the unspoken narratives and beliefs shaping the tension.

- **Engage for conversation, not conversion** – Invite authentic dialogue instead of delivering monologues or ultimatums.

These four moves are deceptively simple. But when used with intention, they change the entire tone, outcome, and emotional temperature of tough conversations.

In this section of the book, you'll get a deep dive into each step. Not just what to do, but why it works—and how to put it into practice. Each chapter is designed to give you both insight and action:

Here's what you can expect in each chapter:

1. **Concept Explanation** – A clear breakdown of what the step means, what it doesn't mean, and why it matters in high-stakes conversations.

2. **Real-Life Applications** – Workplace scenarios, personal conflicts, leadership moments, and even everyday misunderstandings that show how the model works in real life.

3. **Common Misconceptions** – The traps people fall into when trying to "do the right thing"—and what to do instead.

4. **Interactive Exercises** – Prompts, reflections, and real scripts to help you put the model into action.

Each chapter is built to give you tools you can use right now, not just inspiration you'll forget tomorrow.

Why This Matters

Communication is the foundation of leadership, influence, and connection. But when conversations carry weight—when there's emotion, disagreement, or high stakes—most people default to one of three things: avoiding, appeasing, or attacking.

We shrink. We smooth things over. Or we speak with force instead of strategy.

The cost? Misunderstood feedback. Fragile work environments. Tension-filled homes. Missed promotions. Fractured friendships. Silent resentment.

And yet, most of these breakdowns are avoidable—not by changing our personalities, but by changing our approach.

The D.A.R.E. Model gives you that approach.

It's not about being more likable. It's about being more effective. It's not about softening your message. It's about sharpening your clarity and engaging generously.

What You'll Learn (and Practice)

In **Chapter 3**, you'll learn why the words you choose matter and how describing what's happening is more potent than interpreting or assuming. You'll see how small shifts in language can instantly reduce defensiveness and open space for dialogue.

In **Chapter 4**, you'll discover how to find common ground *without* erasing differences. We'll unpack why so many well-intentioned communicators unintentionally shut people down when trying to "bridge the gap" and how to acknowledge someone's experience without abandoning your own.

Chapter 5 will challenge you to examine the stories you're bringing into conversations. Because often, it's not what's being said, but rather what's already been believed. You'll learn to question assumptions that may be clouding your view and how to uncover narratives that fuel unnecessary conflict.

And in **Chapter 6**, we'll land with what may be the most challenging part of all: learning to engage for conversation, not conversion. You'll explore what it looks like to stay in the room, stay curious, and stay connected, even when agreement isn't the primary goal.

This isn't about "talking it out" for the sake of peace. It's about speaking in a way that aligns with your values, goals, and relationships.

Why Now?

In today's world, where conflict is high, patience is low, and clarity is rare, the ability to have honest conversations is no longer optional. It's a competitive advantage. It's a leadership skill. It's a survival tool.

Whether you're building a team culture, managing a crisis, having hard family conversations, or navigating tense social or political moments, your ability to D.A.R.E. makes the difference.

Hey,And it's not about doing it perfectly. It's about being prepared, practiced, and intentional.

So, before you turn the page, take a moment to think about the conversations you've been avoiding. The ones that sit heavy on your chest. The ones you talk about with others but haven't had with the actual person.

This is the framework that will help you move toward those conversations with courage and clarity.

Chapter 3

Describe vs. Interpret: Facts, Feelings, and Fiction

Mei Lin almost ended her marriage over cream cheese.

It was a Saturday morning. Peaceful. Quiet. Birds chirping. Mei Lin had just come back from her 6:30 AM yoga class, where her instructor kept talking about alignment and inner peace. She was feeling good. Her chakras were spinning. Her shoulders were relaxed. Today, she decided, was going to be a "soft life" kind of day.

She walked into the kitchen, pulled out her favorite bagel (the kind she hides in the back of the freezer behind the frozen edamame because she doesn't trust her husband, Greg, not to eat it), popped it in the toaster, and reached for the cream cheese.

Now, here's where the morning's bliss began to crumble.

She opened the fridge and discovered… the full-fat Philadelphia cream cheese was gone.

In its place was one of those sad, passive-aggressive little tubs of "light" cream cheese. The kind that tastes like someone whispered cheese over a container of yogurt.

Mei Lin froze.

Her peaceful yoga energy evaporated in under 0.2 seconds.

This was the same light cream cheese Greg knew she hated. HATED. He knew this. She had ranted about it before. He had apologized before. They'd had a whole argument about how flavorless food is not "healthy," it's punishment. So why… WHY… was this tub in her fridge?

She slammed the fridge. Marched into the bedroom. Crossed her arms.

"Oh, so we're back to this again?" she snapped.

Greg looked up from his phone. "Huh?"

Mei Lin stared. "You replaced my cream cheese with that low-fat nonsense again."

Greg blinked. "I didn't—wait, what? I haven't been to the store in three days."

"Oh, so now it just *magically* appeared in the fridge? Did the dairy fairy drop it off?"

"I don't even eat cream cheese, Mei Lin!"

"Exactly! So why would you buy something you don't even eat unless it was to make a point? You're clearly trying to control what I eat again, and I've told you—"

"Mei Lin. Stop. Breathe."

But Mei Lin was already spiraling. She brought up the time he suggested she order a salad at that barbecue place two years ago. She brought up the keto phase he went through and how he kept putting cauliflower in things that had no business being cauliflowered. She brought up the swimsuit comment from 2021. She was on a roll.

Ten minutes later, she stormed out of the house with a tote bag and a mission: to go to Trader Joe's and buy real cream cheese — the full-fat kind, with dignity and flavor.

And here's the kicker.

While she was gone, Greg texted her a photo.

The photo showed the "light" cream cheese — and next to it, tucked behind the orange juice, an untouched tub of the full-fat kind.

Mei Lin hadn't even looked behind the juice.

She just saw one thing. Interpreted it. Jumped. Assumed motive. Assigned intention. Built a story. And went full courtroom drama.

Mei Lin is You and Me!

While we judged Mei Lin and empathized with her husband, if we are honest, we have all been Mei Lin. Saw one thing, added 15, and ended up in a place of regret. Maybe it wasn't about cream cheese. Maybe it was a side glance in a meeting. A one-word reply in a text. A missed call. A coworker who walked by without speaking. A boss who didn't include you in an email thread. And you created a whole movie in your head. Directed it. Starred in it. Won an Oscar for "Best Performance in a Scene No One Else Was Aware Of."

But here's the deal:

What if you're like Mei Lin?

What if the thing you're mad about isn't even *real* — it's just a story you made up because of your filters?

Our brains are incredible storytellers. But sometimes, they tell the wrong story. When we confuse interpretation for fact, we make decisions, assign blame, and start conflicts based on something that may not even be true.

That's why the first step of the D.A.R.E. model is **Describe.**

Describe means you stick to the observable facts — the things that can be seen, heard, or measured. And, you challenge everything you have labeled as fact to make sure it is not an assumption or interpretation.

Mei Lin's description should have been: "There's a container of light cream cheese in the fridge."

That's it.

Not: "Greg bought this to send me a subtle message."

Not: "He doesn't respect me."

Not: "This is an attack on my personhood and palate."

Just: "There's a tub of light cream cheese in the fridge, and I was looking for the full-fat cream cheese."

Describing keeps us grounded. It keeps us honest. It keeps us from burning the house down over cream cheese.

So, as you read this chapter, I want you to hold onto Mei Lin. Let her be your inner guide. The next time your temperature rises, your assumptions kick in, and your attitude shifts — **pause**.

And here's something important you need to hear:

You can't stop yourself from interpreting.

Seriously. Don't even try.

Your brain is wired for meaning-making. Interpretation isn't a flaw — it's a feature. It's what your mind does to make sense of the world, and honestly, it's protected us for thousands of years.

Imagine a caveman out hunting, watching the tall grass move back and forth as if something large were moving through it. Now, imagine that caveman pausing to say, *"Hmm, do I have enough data to be on guard? I haven't actually seen a sabertooth tiger. I haven't heard one. Maybe I'll just wait until I can confirm for sure. Until then, business as usual."*

That sounds like a dead caveman to me.

So if you think the instruction here is to *never* jump to interpretation, you're wrong.

I want you to gather data, process it through your filter, and come to conclusions. That's how life works.

However — and this is a big however — we usually don't spend *enough* time at the fact-gathering stage before we impose our personal biases and call it "truth."

As we discussed in an earlier chapter, this is how the brain naturally operates. The goal of conversational competence isn't to shut down the brain's natural operation: that's not realistic. You can't stop yourself from interpreting. However, you can catch yourself after the first leap, pause, and take a new pathway.

That's the muscle we're building. Not to pretend interpretation doesn't happen, but to be smart enough not to react blindly to the first story that pops into our head.

Here's how that works:

When you notice you've had an emotional reaction, or you're certain you *know* why someone did something, or you feel yourself getting worked up — **pause**.

Ask yourself: *"How did I get here?"*

Not in a dramatic, 'retrace-my-whole-life-story' kind of way. But in a curious, zoomed-out, *"Wait a minute…"* kind of way.

It's the moment you go from acting on the story to observing the story. You let your interpretation show up — and then you give yourself space to ask: *What was the trigger? What did I see, hear, or notice that made me tell this story?* And more importantly: *Is there another way to look at it?*

That moment of pause? That's the detour. That's the muscle we're building here. That's how you interrupt the default pattern of reacting to your assumptions as if they're reality.

And now — now you're ready to bring in the magic question that rewires the conversation before it even begins:

What are the facts? Have I layered a story on top of the facts?

Because recognizing that leap?

That's the beginning of conversational competence.

That's the start of clarity, connection, and way fewer arguments over dairy products.

Now let's rewind.

Let's imagine that Mei Lin came home from yoga with her peaceful energy *intact*. Let's imagine she remembered the DARE model — specifically **D: Describe** — and gave herself that pause moment.

Same scenario. Same fridge. Same suspicious tub of light cream cheese.

But this time, instead of letting her brain spin a whole drama series in 3.5 seconds, she paused.

She stared at the cream cheese, felt her chest tighten just a bit, and instead of storming into the bedroom like a dairy-crazed thunderstorm, she walked in calmly and said:

"Hey, babe — quick question. I noticed a tub of light cream cheese in the fridge. Did you buy that?"

Greg looked up. "Nope. I haven't even been to the store. Why?"

"Just checking. I looked in the fridge for the regular cream cheese, and all I saw was the light cream cheese. It kind of surprised me, because I hate that flavorless nonsense."

Greg laughed. "I don't mess with your cream cheese. Check behind the juice — maybe your regular one is still in there."

And sure enough, it was.

Crisis averted.

Feelings intact.

Marriage unscathed.

And all because Mei Lin described what she saw, instead of jumping into a story about *why* it was there.

No assumptions. No accusations. No commentary from the peanut gallery in her head. Just a simple observation, shared in a way that left room for truth — not just interpretation.

That, my friend, is what **Describe** looks like in real life.

And if it can save a marriage on a Saturday morning in the kitchen, imagine what it can do in the middle of a high-stakes conversation at work, a disagreement with your teenager, or a conflict with someone you love.

How Assumptions Fuel Unnecessary Arguments

By now, we've spent a lot of time talking about the difference between describing and interpreting. We've seen how a little tub of cream cheese can nearly bring down a marriage, how a missed detail can spark a spiral, and how our brain's reflex to "fill in the blanks" can cause us to react to things that haven't even happened.

But now it's time to ask a deeper question:

What's so wrong with interpretation?

And the answer is… **Absolutely nothing.**

That's right. Interpretation isn't the enemy.

Interpretation is part of how we survive. It's how we read between the lines, how we make decisions quickly, how we gauge danger, opportunity, tone, energy, and intention. It's how we make sense of things that aren't clearly spelled out.

So no — the issue isn't *having* an interpretation.

The issue is the **power we give it** and the **authority we take once we've made it**.

In other words, interpretation becomes dangerous the moment we stop seeing it as a guess and start treating it like a fact.

Where Interpretation Comes From

So let's unpack where all of this comes from.

Interpretation is our brain's way of quickly running a situation through our internal database — our **filters** — and coming up with an answer. Those filters are made of:

- How we were raised
- Our culture and nationality
- Our religion and beliefs
- Our education
- Our past experiences
- What hurt us
- What helped us
- What we've been praised or punished for

Each of us has a unique filter. And we bring that filter into every conversation, whether we mean to or not.

Let me give you a real example from my life.

My mother was in the military. A proud, precise, regulation-driven U.S. Army woman. And she raised me with one very clear message when it came to time:

"To be early is to be on time, to be on time is to be late, and to be late is to be left."

Punctuality was not a suggestion. It was a *value*. Being late was not just inconvenient — it was a sign of disrespect. A moral failing. It meant you didn't care about the other person's time or about keeping your word.

So, what filter did I develop?

That same one. I became the person who gets anxious at 5:45 PM for a 6:00 PM event. I'm triple-checking the route, adjusting for traffic, and setting my shoes by the door. Because to me, being on time doesn't mean *arriving* at 6:00. It means *being at coat check* at 5:45.

But not everyone has that filter.

Same Word, Two Realities

Let's talk about my husband.

He's not late for work. He's not reckless or irresponsible. He's just... *not* raised by an Army mom.

So when we have a social event that starts at 6:00 PM, he's totally fine leaving the house at 6:15. He'll say things like,

"We don't want to be the first ones there."

Meanwhile, I'm pacing like we've already missed a flight.

Now here's where the unnecessary argument comes in.

At 6:05 PM, he's walking around the house with his shoes in his hand, saying, "I'll be ready to go in a few minutes," and I'm already annoyed. Tense. Short in my tone. Huffing and puffing. And he has no idea why.

Because I don't yell, "My momma was in the Army and I was raised to see being late as a sign of disrespect, and I apply that to *everything*."

Nope. What I say is:

"We are late."

And he says:

"We are not late."

And just like that, we are now **arguing over a word** — *late* — that we are both interpreting through completely different filters.

We are using the same vocabulary but living in different dictionaries.

The Real Problem With Interpretation

This is what happens all the time.

We assume everyone else sees the world through our filter. And when they don't? We get offended, frustrated, or confused.

The real problem with interpretation isn't that it happens — it's that **we rarely share the filter we used to get "there"**. We drop conclusions like little landmines in the conversation, expecting the other person to just *know* why we feel the way we feel.

But they can't.

They don't have your backstory. They don't know the tone your father used when he criticized you. They don't know how your teacher made you feel invisible when you were a child. They don't know your internal rules around what respect looks like, what love sounds like, or what effort feels like.

They just know they're being told they're "late."

And now, a conversation that could've been neutral becomes charged.

A moment that could've been clarified turns into a conflict.

Pause: You Have Time

D.A.R.E. is built on the power of the pause.

What gets most conversations on the fast track to chaos isn't just disagreement—it's speed.

We rush in with our interpretations, our feelings, our internal headlines screaming: *"They're wrong!"* or *"They tried the right one!"*

And now, we're reacting to a story we wrote—not what happened.

But here's the thing: **you have time.**

Yes, the conversation needs to happen. Yes, you deserve clarity. But there is no Olympic medal for diving headfirst or finishing the fight fastest.

That moment before you say the thing? That is your window. Pause long enough for your thinking brain to come online.

The pause is not avoidance; it's preparation, and preparation is power.

How Assumptions Turn into Arguments

Let's break it down.

Here's how the escalation happens, step-by-step:

1. **An event happens**

   (We're getting ready for an event that starts at 6:00 PM

2. **You observe something**

   (It's 6:05 PM and he's still not dressed)

3. **You run it through your filter**

   (Late = Disrespect)

4. **You form an interpretation**

   ("He doesn't care about time or me")

5. **You assign intention**

   ("He always does this because he doesn't respect my time and other people. Because of him they will think I am disrespectful."

6. **You react emotionally**

   (Tension, short tone, passive-aggressive remarks)

7. **You say something that seems factual to you, but isn't shared reality**

    "We are late."

8. **The other person responds based on their filter**

    "We are not late."

9. **Now you're arguing over semantics, but underneath is a complete, unspoken belief system.**

    And if you're not aware of it — or willing to pause and break that cycle — it just keeps repeating.

How to Avoid the Trap

So how do we stop assumptions from fueling unnecessary arguments?

1. Recognize your filter.

Know your triggers. Understand what lens you're applying. Ask yourself, "What personal belief is driving this reaction?"

2. Say more than the conclusion.

Instead of just saying, "We're late," try:

"I know this probably doesn't feel late to you, but I get anxious when we're not ready by 5:45 because I was raised to see punctuality as a sign of respect."

Now you're giving context, not just criticism.

3. Get curious about their filter.

Ask: "What does 'on time' mean to you?"

You might be surprised by how many conversations could be solved with a simple question instead of a statement. I tell every student I teach, "When you make a statement, you are setting up for an argument; but when you ask a question, you are setting up for a conversation."

4. Assume difference, not disrespect.

> Most people aren't trying to annoy you — they're just operating on a different rulebook. Don't punish them for not playing by rules they didn't know existed.

Interpretation is natural. It's inevitable. It's human.

The mistake isn't in interpreting — it's in **treating your interpretation as fact**, and then reacting to others as if they already know what you know, believe what you believe, and live by the same rules you do.

When we name our filters, we create clarity. When we hold our interpretations with humility, we create connection. And when we pause long enough to ask, *"Could they be seeing this differently?"*, we prevent a lot of pointless conflicts.

Because when we do all these things? Conversations don't just improve — relationships do too.

Why Knowing Your Triggers is Important

Let's talk about you for a second.

Yes—**you**.

We've spent a lot of time exploring how the "**Describe**" step of the D.A.R.E. model can prevent misunderstandings and help you lead better conversations. But now it's time to turn the mirror around. Because let's be honest: a significant reason we rush to interpret rather than describe is this:

We are *triggered.*

And when we're triggered, we don't want clarity. We want closure. We want a storyline that feels emotionally satisfying and, if we're being real, allows us to feel justified in whatever reaction we're about to serve up.

That's human. But it's also dangerous, especially in high-stakes conversations.

When we're in conflict, what we're experiencing is a collision of values, expectations, experiences, and unspoken histories. Your triggers don't just influence how you feel. They shape the stories you create in your mind about what just happened. And once your brain has filled in the blanks, it treats your interpretation like it's gospel. Not a guess. Not an opinion, but a fact.

That's where things go wrong and why you need to know your triggers.

Triggers and filters are related, but they aren't the same.

Filters shape how you *hear* something. They're the lens through which your past experiences, culture, and beliefs are created, so even neutral words can get distorted. A filter makes you hear "Can we talk?" and assume it's bad news. It's how you interpret.

Triggers, on the other hand, shape how you *react*. They're the emotional hot buttons often formed by pain, fear, shame, or unresolved experiences that cause a surge of emotion or defensiveness, even when the situation doesn't logically warrant it. A trigger bypasses logic and hits your nervous system like an alarm.

When someone brushes up against one of those sore spots, most of us don't pause to check what's happening inside. We just react fast, big, and often without clarity.

Knowing your triggers is about reclaiming control in the moment. Because if you don't recognize them, they'll run the conversation and likely run it straight into the ground.

But here's the good news: knowing your triggers gives you power.

Power to pause. Power to name what's happening. Power to choose your response, not just deliver a reaction.

This is where personal introspection becomes a professional asset. The most effective communicators aren't the ones who never get triggered—they're the ones who **recognize the feeling** and **don't let it hijack the moment**.

Here's what the cycle often looks like when we're unaware of our triggers:

- **Something happens**

  A colleague interrupts you during a meeting.

- **You feel something**

  A flash of irritation, a pang of disrespect. You've been here before.

- **You assign meaning**

  They're trying to dominate the conversation. They don't think I'm competent. They always do this to me because I'm the only finance person on the team.

- **You react**

  You cut them off later in the meeting. You shut down. You vent to a coworker. You withdraw. And, hopefully, not all in the same meeting.

But here's what might be true:

They thought you had finished your point.

They were trying to build on your idea.

They're socially awkward and interrupt everyone—nothing personal.

When we aren't aware of our triggers, we interpret *with bias*, and often in a way that doesn't serve us. We cast ourselves as the victim, the disrespected, the overlooked. And it's not that those feelings are invalid or even false, but we have not stopped to ground them in fact.

Knowing your triggers helps you create space between **what happened** and **what you think it means**. And that space is where mature, effective communication lives.

How to find your Triggers

You probably already know your major ones—those things that consistently make your blood boil or send you into shutdown mode. But sometimes they hide in plain sight. Here's a simple exercise to surface them:

Reflect:

- What behaviors or comments consistently provoke a strong reaction in you?

- When do you find it hardest to stay calm and curious?

- What situations bring out a version of you that even you don't like or know is not best equipped to handle the situation?

Pattern-spot:

Look for themes. Is it always when someone questions your authority? When someone ignores your contributions? When you feel excluded? When someone makes you feel like you're back in that old job where your ideas weren't valued?

Name it:

Once you've identified a trigger, give it a name. Write it down. Say it out loud. Treat it like a GPS warning you about a detour ahead—not something to fear, but something to navigate consciously.

Governing your response:

Let's go back to the meeting example. Say your trigger is someone interrupting or talking over you. You're in a team meeting, and someone louder than you cuts you off or redirects your idea. Your body tightens. That familiar frustration creeps in. You want to shut down—or speak up with heat.

But this time, you pause.

You say to yourself: *This is one of my triggers. Let me describe first, then ask for clarity.*

Instead of, "Why do you always interrupt me?"

You try:

"I noticed I was sharing an idea, and it was redirected before I finished. I would like to revisit it and finish. I think it is valuable to this conversation."

See the difference? You've acknowledged the moment without accusation. You've protected your dignity *and* left room for conversation. That's what it looks like to govern your response.

The outcome you create:

You don't just want to be right. You want to be effective. And that means choosing words and actions that help you express your experience without burning a bridge, understand the other person, and stay in the conversation.

When you know your triggers, you give yourself the chance to do that, because you'll recognize when your nervous system is trying to hand you a script based on past pain. And you can choose a better one.

Not because you're suppressing your truth.But because you're *owning your response.*

Chapter 3 Recap: Describe vs. Interpret — *The Cream Cheese Catastrophe*

Cliff Notes, Dethra-Styles

Mei Lin went from downward dog to emotional detonation over a tub of light cream cheese. Why? Because she saw something, interpreted it as sabotage, and let her imagination do a high-speed chase through every unresolved issue in her marriage. Spoiler alert: the full-fat cream cheese was behind the orange juice the whole time.

Moral of the story? **Don't let your feelings write fiction and call it fact.**

Key Takeaways:

- Your brain is wired to interpret—it's not wrong, just needs a pause button.

- The **Describe** step is all about stating what you *saw, heard,* or *noticed* without layering on meaning.

- Interpretation becomes harmful when we treat it like the truth instead of a hypothesis.

- Filters like culture, upbringing, trauma, and values influence how we interpret everything.

- Triggers amplify our tendency to jump to conclusions and must be managed with intention.

- Knowing your triggers allows you to pause, reframe, and show up better in high-stakes conversations.

Ask yourself: What did I observe? What story am I telling about it?

Why This Matters:

Miscommunication doesn't start with what people do—it starts with what we *think* it means. Most workplace drama, relationship friction, and even self-doubt stem from unexamined interpretations that feel like facts. This chapter is your cheat code for pulling the plug on unnecessary conflict by separating what's real from what's assumed. It's not about ignoring your gut—it's about confirming the facts before launching a full-blown response.

Call to Action:

Pause the next time you're triggered. Before you speak, ask: *Am I describing or interpreting?* Then choose language or pose a question that leaves space for clarity, not just catharsis. And if you need inspiration, channel your inner Mei Lin... *and look behind the juice.*

Interactive Exercise: Practice Describing Without Interpreting

Let's bring this home.

You've just learned that interpretation isn't bad, but it needs a seatbelt. You've seen how filters shape the way we react. You've watched Mei Lin and my Army-mama clock trauma play out in real time.

Now it's your turn.

Because knowing the difference between **describe** and **interpret** is powerful — but *practicing it* is where fundamental transformation begins. This quick exercise will help you slow down your reactions, catch your filters in action, and build the muscle of description-first communication.

THE EXERCISE: "Just the Facts, Friend"

Grab a piece of paper or open a notes app.

Step 1: Think of a recent moment that irritated, hurt, or confused you.
It could be at work, with your partner, a family member, or even a stranger.

Choose a moment where you felt tension or assumed something about the other person's behavior.

Step 2: Write out what happened as a *description only*. Stick to what could have been seen or heard — like a video camera with no captions, thoughts, or voiceover.

Example: "He walked in at 9:17 AM, did not make eye contact, and sat down silently."

Step 3: Now write out your initial *interpretation* of that moment. Be honest — what did you *think* it meant?

Example: "He's mad at me. He's avoiding me. He thinks I messed up the report."

Step 4: Ask yourself: "What filter did I apply to reach that conclusion?" Was it about tone? Past experience? A belief you hold about how people "should" behave?

Step 5: Challenge yourself to write at least two *other* interpretations that could also be true. This flexes your perspective muscle.

Example: "Maybe he was distracted by something personal. Maybe he's just tired. Maybe he didn't even notice I was there."

THE DEBRIEF

This exercise may seem simple, but it's a game-changer.

It reveals just how fast — and how automatically — we jump to conclusions. It also shows how little information we sometimes have when we decide what someone's actions *mean*.

Here's the deeper insight: the facts don't change. What changes is the meaning we assign to them.

And the more you practice separating the description from the interpretation, the more clarity you create in your conversations. You become more emotionally regulated. You ask better questions. You react with less fire and more focus.

Most importantly, you stop arguing about things that aren't even happening.

Chapter 4

Acknowledge – The Balance Between Finding Common Ground and Respecting Differences

It started with the pants.

Bright yellow. Plaid. Suspiciously high water. The kind of pants that made you squint and ask yourself, "Is this... a fashion risk or a cry for help?"

My coworker, Marcus, walked into the office as if it were just another Tuesday. He had paired the pants with a polka-dot button-down, mismatched socks, and a tie that looked like it had been borrowed from a ventriloquist dummy. Not a single thread was vibing with the others. He looked like a bag of Skittles.

But the rest of us? We said nothing. Not a peep. We smiled, nodded, complimented the coffee, and carried on with our lives like we weren't in the presence of wardrobe chaos.

About fifteen minutes later, just before we were supposed to walk into a meeting with senior execs, Marcus busted out laughing and said:

"So you really weren't going to acknowledge that I looked crazy? You were just gonna let me walk in there like this?!"

We laughed too, mostly in relief that we hadn't somehow entered the post-fashion apocalypse. But then I said:

"Listen, I saw the tie. I saw the pants. But I figured maybe it was one of those 'expressions over conformity' moments, and I didn't want to minimize what could've been a bold statement just because it was different from his usual business casual."

And in that moment, it hit me. That's how we treat conversations, too.

We see the difference. We feel the tension. And instead of naming it, we smooth over it with politeness or pretend it's not there, just in case what someone's wearing (or saying or doing) is a statement, not a mistake.

But acknowledgment doesn't mean disrespect. It doesn't mean judgment. It just means, "I see it." And that's where real connection starts.

When we say, "Acknowledge similarities without minimizing differences," we need to break that down.

Let's start with what **Acknowledge** means in the context of the D.A.R.E. model. It's not about nodding politely, pretending to listen, or offering hollow empathy. And it's not even about agreeing with the other person.

The "A" in D.A.R.E. isn't about acknowledging *the person*. It's about acknowledging *the difference*.

Yes, people need to be acknowledged; that's basic human decency. We owe each other presence and a little bit of humanity. If that's a foreign concept, conversational competence might not be your first step.

What we're talking about here is different.In D.A.R.E., acknowledgment is about recognizing that in any real conversation, there's more than one truth, more than one experience, and more than one perspective that matters.

This distinction is crucial. Because when most people hear "acknowlededge," they think it means agreement or affirmation. But that's not the goal here.

The goal is to validate the presence and relevance of differences in the conversation, without minimizing, erasing, or steamrolling it just to keep things comfortable.

Why This Matters

Human beings are hardwired to seek safety and comfort. That comfort, especially when dealing with other people, is often found in the things we share in common— common ground. It feels safe. It's stabilizing. It sends the message, "You're like me and like me is not a threat," and, more subtly, "We don't need to change too much to get along."

From a neurological standpoint, similarity is soothing. Research from the University of Virginia using MRI brain scans found that when people perceive others as similar to themselves, the brain responds to their pain and pleasure as if it were their own. But when faced with someone perceived as different, that neural empathy drops significantly.

Translation: Our brains make it easier to care when we feel alike. And that means we often rush to find sameness *at the expense of understanding and resolving differences.*

The Comfort Trap

We all crave comfort, especially in tense conversations. It's why people say things like:

- "We're all human."
- "I don't see color/disability/gender."
- "At the end of the day, we all want the same things."

These phrases sound kind. Inclusive, even. But often, they function as escape hatches, ways to avoid engaging with what makes someone else's experience fundamentally different.

Here's the problem: You can't solve a problem you're unwilling to see.

And you can't understand a person if you refuse to understand the filter through which they live.

Real-Life Example: Arielle and Dan

This brings us to a real-life moment at a leadership retreat hosted by my ExecuPrep team for a Fortune 500 company. The kind of event where participants shuffle into conference rooms with paper name tags and refillable coffee mugs, prepped for workshops on communication and connection.

Dan, a mid-50s regional executive, was paired with Arielle, a sharp, funny woman in her early 40s who uses a wheelchair. Their task: share something meaningful about themselves and discuss how their identities have shaped their leadership.

Dan started with his upbringing, a working-class family, and a first-generation college graduate. Arielle nodded, sharing how being raised by working-class parents shaped her drive, and how her accident in her twenties redefined her relationship with independence.

They found surface-level common ground. They both liked dogs. Both mentored younger professionals. Both had been underestimated early in their careers.

Each time Arielle spoke, Dan jumped in with:

- "Same here!"

- "I know exactly what you mean."

- "That's just like me!"

It was clear that Dan was trying to make her feel comfortable. However, it was also clear that he was trying to make *himself* feel at ease.

Then came the moment.

Dan leaned forward and said, "Honestly, I don't even see you as a woman in a wheelchair. I just see you as a great leader." He meant it as a compliment.

But Arielle didn't smile. She gently replied:

"I need you to see this wheelchair. Because if you don't see it, you won't understand how I navigate this building, this company, or this world. And if you can't see it, you won't know when or how I may need your help, or where you have power that I don't."

Dan froze. The air shifted.

And that's when their conversation actually began.

See the Difference

When Dan said he didn't "see" Arielle as a woman in a wheelchair, what he meant was: "I'm trying not to treat you differently."

But what she heard, and what many hear in similar situations, was: "Your difference makes me uncomfortable and I'm unwilling to engage with your lived experience."

The difference wasn't the problem.

The *denial* of difference was.

And this is where we often go wrong.

We assume that focusing on similarities will make hard conversations easier. We hope that by emphasizing sameness, the discomfort of difference will subside. But that's not how resolution works.

You can't move through conflict by pretending it's not there. You can't solve for friction by ignoring the factors that caused it. And you can't lead cross-functional teams, build inclusive environments, or engage in meaningful dialogue without learning to acknowledge and appreciate differences.

The Data Behind Difference

This isn't just theoretical.

A 2017 Deloitte report on diversity and inclusion found that employees in organizations with inclusive cultures are 42% less likely to leave their jobs in a year and 80% more likely to believe their organization is high-performing. But inclusion isn't created by blanket sameness. It's created when people feel their specific identities are seen, valued, and understood.

Similarly, research published in *The Journal of Experimental Social Psychology* found that multicultural approaches — those that acknowledge and engage with differences — lead to stronger team collaboration and higher individual performance than colorblind or sameness-focused approaches.

In short? Pretending we don't disagree just because we agree on most things isn't real agreement, and it's definitely not progress. It's avoidance dressed up as harmony. And it keeps us from doing the real work: having the hard conversations that lead to resolution, collaboration, and shared outcomes.

Getting Comfortable with Discomfort

Let's be clear: acknowledging difference doesn't just mean identity-based differences. Yes, we used the Arielle and Dan story as a visual; it's memorable and easy to wrap your mind around. But this chapter is about something deeper and more applicable to your everyday work life.

It's about acknowledging where you and someone else don't see the issue the same way, and not letting that difference derail the conversation.

Because in real life, breakdowns are not always identity-based. They happen over deadlines, performance reviews, project direction, and promotion conversations. They happen when one person thinks "We're behind," and the other thinks "We're pacing just fine." When one person says, "This team isn't performing," and the other hears, "I'm being blamed." When your version of fair doesn't match theirs.

Acknowledging those differences can feel risky. You might worry about escalating the situation. You might be afraid you'll make it worse. You might think, "If I point out how far apart we are, we'll never get back on track." But here's the truth: you can't fix what you won't name, you can't solve a conflict you're too afraid to acknowledge, and you can't communicate effectively by skipping over the friction.

Acknowledging difference, in perspective, in expectations, in interpretation, isn't about blame. It's about clarity. And clarity is where resolution begins.

So what does acknowledgment look like in a real conversation?

It sounds like:

- "We're seeing this differently, and I want to understand where you're coming from."

- "It sounds like this didn't land the way I thought it would. Can we unpack that?"

- "We're not aligned here, but I'm committed to finding a way forward."

It is a choice between the harder path of transparency and the easier path of false agreement. It appears that recognizing that comfort and clarity don't always arrive at the same time, but if you want better outcomes, clarity must come first. Because when you skip the hard part to keep the peace, you don't get peace. You just delay the conflict until it explodes somewhere less convenient.

The Biggest Mistakes People Make When Trying to "Bridge the Gap"

When people try to build bridges in conversation, they usually do so with good intentions. They're trying to be inclusive. They're trying to de-escalate. They're trying to find common ground. However, good intentions don't always translate to effective communication, especially when you're skipping steps or bypassing the truth.

Let me show you what I mean.

Quick Story: The Performance Review That Went Sideways

Jenna was conducting Malik's annual review. He'd had a solid year, creative contributions, a strong rapport with teammates, and positive outcomes across most projects. However, there was one high-visibility assignment that went off track. The deadline was missed, the budget was blown, and leadership took notice.

Jenna wanted to give him strong, actionable feedback without making him feel like a failure, so she said, "Hey, I've definitely missed deadlines before, too. We're all juggling a lot. It happens."

Malik nodded, visibly relieved, because he *knew* how badly the project had gone and how much heat leadership had generated behind closed doors. He walked out thinking, "Okay, cool. Everyone gets that things like this happen. I'll bounce back. No big deal."

Except it *was* a big deal.

Not only did leadership notice, but several people had to put their reputations on the line just to protect Malik's job. The delay had rattled trust at the top and nearly tanked a major opportunity.

Jenna didn't *mean* to minimize it. But in her effort to find common ground, she left Malik with the wrong takeaway. He didn't hear, "I don't want you to feel like a failure, but this can't happen again." He heard, "It happens." And just like that, the moment for growth and accountability was gone.

Let's Break It Down:

Jenna was trying to connect. She reached for empathy to soften the blow.

But in doing so, she blurred the message, and that might have caused more damage to Malik's career than a hard truth ever could.

Her mistake?

Trying so hard to make the feedback feel safe that she inadvertently downplayed/ unintentionally minimized the severity and consequences of Malik's derailed assignment, leaving the most essential part of the feedback unsaid.

And she's not alone.

Here are some of the most common mistakes people make when they're trying to "bridge the gap" in conversation.

Mistake #1: Rushing to Similarity

People jump to statements like:

"We've all been there."

"The same thing happened to me."

"That happens to everyone."

Why it doesn't work:

It skips over the other person's unique context and assumes sameness equals understanding. But *sameness is not the same as specificity,*and real acknowledgment requires specificity.

Just because we're in the same situation doesn't mean we share the same experience or outcomes.

Let's say both of us check our bank accounts and the balance says $20. That's it. That's all.

I look at it and panic. You look at it and decide to treat yourself to a $15 lunch.

Which one of us is being unreasonable? Neither.

Because for me, that might be my *last* $20. You? You might have a savings account, a money market account, a spending account at another bank, a royalty check scheduled to hit tomorrow morning, and a generous relative who randomly drops cash in your account when your balance dips.

Same situation: $20 in the checking account: totally different reality.

So before you assume your story matches theirs, pause.

Try this instead:

"I've had a similar experience, but I also know yours is different. Can you tell me more about how it played out for you?"

Mistake #2: Dismissing Emotion with Logic

Let's pause for a second, because if you've already read Chapter 3, you might be thinking, "Wait, didn't you tell me to *Describe instead of interpret*? Aren't facts and data safer than assumptions and emotions?"

Yes... and no.

Describe versus interpret is about resisting the urge to assign meaning before you have the facts. But here's the thing: Describing doesn't mean dehumanizing.

Facts are powerful, but they don't exist in a vacuum. When someone brings emotion, frustration, or vulnerability into a conversation and you respond with charts, policy, or "Here's the spreadsheet," you're not solving the problem; you're skipping the connection.

You're not wrong. You're just not being helpful.

Some people default to logic or policy because it feels safe. It keeps things "professional". But what they feel is that they are in control.

Let's stop here and dispel this longstanding myth that emotions are not professional. Have you ever disliked a project, like a boss, got angry at a work scenario, or felt happy because a project went well? Dislike, like, anger, and joy are all emotions that we experience every single day at work.

Emotions are not unprofessional; how we demonstrate them can be. For example, it is professional to be excited that your boss advocated for you and the finance department approved the budget for your pet project. It may be unprofessional, however, if you respond to happiness by running across the room, jumping into your boss's arms, wrapping your legs around their waist, and asking to be spun around, like a scene from a Broadway musical. We all have emotions at work, but we are not all comfortable including them in the conversation, especially when we are unsure of how to navigate them or the potential fissures they may reveal.

Ignoring the emotion does not communicate control. But what it often communicates is, "I hear your feelings, but I don't respect them enough to respond to them."

That's not acknowledgment; that's a power play disguised as practicality.

Quick Scenario: The Project Pushback

During a team check-in, Jackson opened up about feeling burned out and disrespected. Deadlines were moving with no warning, workload was piling up, and the pressure was starting to impact his mental health.

His manager nodded and said:

"I hear you. However, based on our workload projections and resource allocation, this is the current reality. We all have to adjust."

Technically? She wasn't wrong. Emotionally? She might as well have said, "Toughen up and deal with it."

Jackson didn't feel seen. He felt dismissed, and after that meeting, he stopped speaking up altogether and began his search for another role.

Why it doesn't work?

When someone brings up a concern or disagreement, leading with logic can feel like you're bulldozing their experience. It sends the message:

"This isn't valid unless it fits neatly into a policy document or aligns with my ideals."

And let's be realistic, most workplace conflicts aren't rooted in facts. It's rooted in how those facts make us feel.

Reality: My project budget was cut

Feeling: I don't have enough resources to deliver the quality of work my boss expects.

Reality: My co-worker was terminated in the Reduction In Force

Feeling: I might be reduced next, despite being reassured that I will not.

Facts evoke feelings, and that is really what we are discussing in most instances.

Try this instead:

Jackson's boss could have responded with, "That sounds incredibly frustrating. Let's break this down together so we can figure out what's fixable."

Because acknowledging the emotion isn't weakness, it's wisdom, and emotional intelligence is the difference between being technically correct and being conversationally competent.

Mistake #3: Confusing Validation with Agreement

This one trips a lot of people up, especially leaders. It's the moment when someone says, 'I hear you,' and the other person assumes that means, 'I agree with you.' But validation isn't the same as endorsement—and that misunderstanding can derail the whole conversation.

They think, "If I acknowledge this, it means I'm admitting fault. And I didn't even do anything wrong."

So instead of leaning in, they stay silent or they try to fast-forward through the conversation with a vague "Let's just move forward."

Why it doesn't work?

Acknowledgment doesn't equal agreement, so you can recognize someone's frustration, their experience, or the fact that something went wrong without claiming responsibility for what caused the problem. But when you skip that recognition, you don't just lose trust, you lose the focus of the conversation.

Let's talk about that for a second: losing the focus of the conversation. This is important because this part gets messy.

Have you ever been in an argument where, at some point, the conversation got so off track that you had to stop and say, "Wait… what are we even arguing about right now?"

That happened because someone made **Mistake #3**: they didn't want to take ownership, and the other person needed acknowledgement. So, instead

99

of discussing the actual issue at hand, the conversation shifted to *what they couldn't move past– the very thing they needed acknowledged.* You were trying to move forward, and they were stuck at the stop sign of "You haven't acknowledged what happened." And until that's named, the conversation won't go anywhere productive.

Quick Scenario: *The New Boss and the Old Mess*

Dev had been burned. His former manager promised him a promotion, dangled it for nearly a year like it was already his, then gave it to someone else without warning or explanation.

Three months later, Shawn stepped in as the new manager. And while he inherited the role, he also inherited the baggage that came with it: side-eyes in meetings, lukewarm hellos, and a team full of polite distrust. Dev was the most vocal.

During a one-on-one, Dev finally said, "I just don't trust what I'm being told anymore. I was about to leave the company, and to keep me, I was promised the next promotion. Then I was blindsided when the role was given to someone who had less time in the position, lower productivity, and fewer results. So when you say things like 'just hang in there,' all I can think is: *I don't have any hang left in me.*"

Shawn froze. He hadn't made any promises, and he wasn't the one who strung Dev along. So he said, "Well, that wasn't me, and there is nothing I can do about that. I can't speak to what happened before I got here."

Technically? He was right. Relationally? He had just told Dev, "That's not my problem."

Dev responded, "Understood."

But, Dev left the meeting, checked out, and disengaged, "Cool. My next move is out."

Try this instead:

Shawn could have said, "I can see how that situation left a bad taste. That kind of letdown would make anyone skeptical. I reviewed your record, and I see that you are a valuable employee that I don't want to lose. My goal is to rebuild that trust, not brush past what happened, so let's talk about what that looks like for you."

Why this works:

It validates the emotional residue of the past without assuming blame. It positions the new leader as someone committed to repair, not retreat, and it keeps the conversation focused, not on rehashing the past, but on *what comes next.*

Because in high-stakes conversations, especially where trust has been broken, people don't always need you to fix the past, but they do need you to recognize that it happened and that it matters.

Mistake #4: Overpersonalizing the Moment

This happens when someone turns the conversation into their own story. A team member brings up a tough experience, and suddenly the other person jumps in with, "That reminds me of the time I..."

And just like that, the spotlight shifts. The gap hasn't been bridged; it's been paved over with a story the other person didn't ask for.

And remember: this isn't a competition for who's endured the toughest experience or the worst company story. It's an opportunity to engage with the person and perspective for greater connection, understanding, and resolution.

Quick Scenario: The Budget Cut Blindside

During a team debrief, Mateo opened up about how demoralizing it felt to find out that two roles on his team had been cut without warning. He had just spent weeks building a roadmap with those people in mind. He felt blindsided, out of the loop, and undervalued.

Before he could even finish his story, his colleague Bryan jumped in, "Oh man, that reminds me of when my team got hit with layoffs during COVID.

I had to deliver the news *virtually,* and one of my direct reports started crying in front of everyone. It was the most awkward moment of my career."

Was Bryan trying to connect? Sure. But what Mateo heard was, "Let me top your pain with mine."

Instead of acknowledgment, Mateo got a plot twist, and now the conversation was about Bryan, while his issue was left unheard and unaddressed.

Why it doesn't work?

Overpersonalizing the moment shifts the focus. The conversation has been hijacked by a story no one asked for and is not helpful.

Have you ever told someone you were sick, and suddenly it turned into a "Who Had It Worse?" competition?

This happens a *lot* with childbirth stories. Everyone who's ever given birth is probably laughing right now because, at some point, they've either participated in or witnessed a "my labor was worse than yours" showdown. And just when they thought the crown had been claimed, someone who's passed a kidney stone enters the chat like, "Well, my doctor said passing a kidney stone is *exactly like* giving birth."

And now what were we even talking about?

You got pulled into the drama of labor and kidney stones, and now you're either completely off track or silently asking yourself, "Wait, what was her point again?"

That's precisely what happens when someone overpersonalizes a conversation: you lose the thread. You miss the point. You derail the moment.

It feels like a connection to the person doing the derailing, but it often feels like a distraction or dismissal to the person who needs to be heard. We do it because we're trying to show the other person they're not alone, trying to comfort them by saying, "Hey, I've been there too."

And let's be honest: similarity is comforting. It feels safe. Familiar. Human.

But sometimes, in trying to offer comfort, we accidentally take over the conversation. So rather than bridge the gap, we build a detour.

Try this instead:

"I understand. Tell me more."

Because sometimes the most powerful thing you can say in a conversation is *less.*

The Real Bridge

True bridge-building doesn't come from minimizing differences. It comes from naming it, respecting it, and then reaching across it. Acknowledging similarity is helpful, but only when you also honor the difference that's shaping how each person sees the conversation.

Because in high-stakes communication performance reviews, promotion discussions, team tension it's not just about finding what you have in common it's about creating enough conversational safety to tell the truth about what you don't.

Chapter 4 Recap: Acknowledge – The Balance Between Finding Common Ground and Respecting Differences

Cliff Notes, Dethra-Style

Similarities make us comfortable; differences make us pause. And when we're in a tough conversation, our natural instinct is to reach for comfort. That instinct shows up as quick compromises, vague affirmations, and most commonly, false agreement.

False agreement occurs when we say, *"Well, we agree on almost everything,"* and move on, conveniently ignoring the fact that the areas where you are not aligned are likely the most critical pieces of the conversation.

In other words, we seek unity at the cost of clarity and resolution. And that costs us more than we realize.

A 2019 Harvard Business Review study found that teams that regularly engaged in productive disagreement outperformed those that avoided conflict by 25% in decision quality and team performance. Why? Because facing difference, without minimizing it, is the launchpad for real progress.

Acknowledging someone's perspective in a conversation does not mean you're agreeing with them. It doesn't mean you're backing down, giving in, or turning in your leadership badge. And it definitely doesn't mean you're saying, *"You're right and I'm wrong."* It simply means you're committed to conversational competence: the ability to navigate complexity, disagreement, and discomfort without compromising truth or relationship.

Key Takeaways:

- **Acknowledgment ≠ Agreement**

  You can acknowledge someone's frustration, experience, or concern without endorsing their conclusions.

- **Similarity is comforting but can be misleading**

  Reaching for common ground too quickly can cause us to skip over the root of the issue.

- **False agreement keeps us stuck**

  When we pretend to agree just to maintain the peace, we miss an opportunity to address the real issue. The illusion of alignment can block the path to resolution.

- **Four common mistakes people make when trying to bridge the gap:**

  1. **Rushing to similarity** – Avoiding discomfort by focusing only on what's shared.

  2. **Dismissing emotion with logic** – Offering data when the person needs empathy.

  3. **Confusing validation with agreement** – Avoiding acknowledgment to protect your position.

  4. **Overpersonalizing the moment** – Shifting the conversation to your story and missing theirs.

- **You don't have to lose your voice to respect someone else's**

  It is possible and powerful to say, *"I see where you're coming from,"* and still hold your position. Conversational competence isn't about winning every point; it's about keeping the conversation alive long enough to find real solutions.

Why This Matters

This chapter wasn't just about navigating conversations across lines of identity (though we did touch on that). It was about what happens when you and someone else see a situation differently, and you still need to move forward together.

Whether it's a project conversation, a peer disagreement, or a performance review, this ability to acknowledge difference without defensiveness is the core skill that separates conflict avoiders from conflict navigators.

According to the 2023 State of Workplace Communication Report, 79% of employees experience tension with colleagues, and 73% say poor communication contributes directly to project failure. Acknowledgment is one of the fastest ways to prevent that breakdown.

This chapter gave you the tools to prevent communication from becoming combat.

It helped you recognize:

- When you're prioritizing comfort over clarity

- When you're softening the message too much

- When you're making someone else's moment about you

- And when you're skipping acknowledgment altogether, it looks like you are taking blame

It taught you to say:

"That wasn't my intention, but I hear how it landed."

"I still believe this was the right call, and I can also understand how it affected you."

"We're not aligned yet, but I want to stay in this conversation."

Because here's the truth:

Acknowledgment isn't surrender. It's a solid strategy for building a bridge. And the best communicators, the ones who lead, influence, and inspire, use that strategy well.

Call to Action:

Let's not just reflect. Let's act.

This week, I want you to practice one moment of intentional acknowledgment, especially in a situation where you disagree with the other person or didn't cause the problem.

You don't need a major conflict to try this. Look for moments like:

- A teammate who's frustrated about a change you didn't control

- A colleague who's still hurt by something that happened before you joined the project

A direct report who feels left out, even though it wasn't your decision.

When that moment arises, try one of the phrases we practiced:

"I wasn't here when that happened, but I understand why it's left an impact."

"That sounds like it caught you off guard. I want to understand more before we move forward."

"I didn't intend for it to land that way, but I can hear that it did and that matters."

Then pause. Let it land. And listen.

That's where trust begins to rebuild, collaboration gets real, and where difference turns from division into direction.

This is where you demonstrate your commitment to effective communication and shared results, which must include acknowledgment.

Chapter 5

Review the Narrative(s) You Have Accepted as Fact

Here's a wild thought: Most of what you "know" isn't knowledge. It's inherited thought: you didn't gain it from experience or education, someone told you it was true, and you navigated life trusting what you were told..

That's not an insult, it's psychology. According to researchers, up to 95% of our daily thoughts, emotions, and behaviors are driven by the subconscious — a mental storage unit filled with beliefs, assumptions, and stories we didn't consciously choose. We absorbed them.

From parents, teachers, church, sitcoms, and the office gossip. From every "that's just how it is" we heard before we were old enough to question it.

So when someone says something that doesn't line up with our version of truth, we rarely stop to ask, "What made them think that?" Nope. We go straight to: "Who raised you?" "They've clearly lost their mind." "People these days…"

Welcome to the "R" in DARE: **Review.**

It's about taking a closer look at your internal operating system and asking,

"Wait… did I install that on purpose? Or did it come preloaded?"

This is not the part where we burn it all down. It's not about becoming someone else or rejecting everything you've ever believed. Instead, it's about slowing down enough to examine the script: some of it handwritten by your grandmother, some of it downloaded from the media, some of it was assigned to you by the world before you even knew how to spell "society."

And then asking,

"Is this accurate?"

"Is this current?"

"Is this even mine?"

Because here's the honest truth: **deeply held beliefs shape the way we communicate, and not always for the better.**

When someone challenges your "facts," it rarely feels like a conversation. It feels like an attack.

Your guard goes up. Your tone shifts. You say, "I'm just being honest," but what you really mean is, "I'm protecting a belief I didn't know I had."

And that's why this chapter matters.

If we don't review the stories running our internal dialogue, we end up defending unexamined narratives as if they were facts and jeopardizing the possibility of collaboration, conflict resolution, and shared results. Narratives that were never accurate. Narratives that might've been true once but are long expired. Narratives designed for survival are killing our relationships.

Now let me bring this home with a story that's not academic, political, or even controversial.

It's just… a woman, a pair of jeans, and a post-baby identity crisis in front of a mirror.

A Closet Full of Narratives

I have been athletic for most of my life, participating in dance, drill team, marching band, and track and field. My body has always done what I asked it to do, especially when it came to my appearance. If I wanted to tone up a little for a vacation where I would spend 98% of my time in a bikini, I just did a few extra crunches here and there, and voilà. I had a narrative, a deeply held belief, that I never questioned because it never had a reason to: I was a size 4, my clothes fit, and my body looked a certain way. End of Discussion.

Then marriage, 41 weeks, and a second baby.

Now, let me pause here and say that no one prepared me for this part. Yes, people talk about getting your body back, but they never tell you that you might come home, stand in front of the mirror, and have a full-blown argument with yourself while trying to button a pair of jeans that used to only need one or two jumps to slide on and fit like a glove.

I stood there, struggling with a zipper and a truth I didn't want to face. My body had changed– I was no longer the size 4 I had been for nearly 10 years– but my narrative had not changed.

And let's be clear, it wasn't about my size. It was about the story I was still telling myself. My story was, "Without a baby inside me, I'm a size 4." A story that was once accurate, but is no longer current. It had expired, and I hadn't taken the time to **Review** it and embrace a new story. Why? Because that story was too closely tied to who I believed I was. Letting it go felt like losing a piece of my identity, just because some jeans (that had clearly shrunk in the closet, mind you) refused to button or zip up.

But instead of reviewing my narrative, I went on a denim expedition, trying on every pair of jeans in the closet. Not because I didn't know the truth, but because I refused to accept it. Surely, the problem was the pants, not the narrative I was clinging to.

That's what narratives do. They sneak into your identity, tuck themselves behind your values, and then whisper to you in conversations:

"You're right. They're wrong."

"You don't need to explain. They should understand."

"You already know how this ends. Don't bother asking questions.
"You are still a size 4; those jeans shrank."

Narratives Are Powerful, and Not Always True

Think about this:

If I asked, *"Why did Rosa Parks become a civil rights icon?"* Most people would say, *"Because she was tired and refused to give up her seat."*

That's the story most of us were taught. And on the surface, it feels powerful: a quiet act of defiance that sparked a movement.

But here's the thing, it's only part of the story. And when we don't review the story, we miss the power of what actually happened.

Rosa Parks wasn't just a tired seamstress. She was the **secretary of the Montgomery chapter of the NAACP**, a seasoned activist, and someone who had been trained in civil disobedience. Her decision wasn't random; it was strategic. It was *planned*. She was part of a movement that had been laying the groundwork for months.

And she wasn't even the first Black woman in Montgomery to refuse to give up her seat. That was **Claudette Colvin**, a 15-year-old who did it months earlier but was deemed "too controversial" by civil rights leaders at the time because she was young, dark-skinned, and pregnant.

So... what's the truth?

It depends on which narrative you were handed. The tidy one that fits inside a fourth-grade history book? Or the complex, messy, but far more empowering version that centers strategy, identity, and the reality of how movements actually work?

When we don't **Review**, we cling to stories that feel good instead of stories that are true.

And when we bring those incomplete narratives into our conversations, especially across lines of difference, we don't just miscommunicate, we misunderstand each other at the most fundamental level.

Your Turn

Right now, I want you to pause and ask yourself:

- What stories do I tell myself about who I am, what I deserve, or how people should treat me?
- Where did those stories come from?
- And when was the last time I reviewed them?

Let's be clear: some of your narratives used to be true. Some still are. And some need to be updated, like an expired passport.

How Deeply Held Beliefs Shape How We Communicate (for Better or Worse)

We all come into conversations with baggage. But it's not always the kind you can see or name. Sometimes the most influential thing in the room isn't the person speaking, it's the invisible script they're following. These scripts, also known as deeply held beliefs or narratives, shape how we perceive ourselves, how we expect others to behave, and how we respond when they fail to meet our expectations.

They're the silent directors of our internal dialogue and the loud megaphones behind our external reactions.

What Are Deeply Held Beliefs?

Let's break it down.

A **deeply held belief** is a story you've accepted as true, often without questioning it. These beliefs can come from:

- Family traditions ("Our people don't air dirty laundry.")
- Cultural norms ("Respect your elders, no matter what.")
- Educational systems ("Success looks like straight A's and a college degree.")
- Religious teachings ("If you have enough faith...")
- Media and popular culture ("Beauty is a size X.")
- Workplace mantras ("If you work hard, keep your head down, go above and beyond, and let your work speak for you, you'll be rewarded.")

They become the internal voice that has been talking so long that you don't even recognize it is always telling you a story.

These beliefs aren't inherently bad. Some are helpful. They give us stability, identity, and a sense of belonging. However, problems arise when they go **unreviewed**, when we carry them into every conversation like a universal truth, expecting others to honor and abide by them.

And when they don't? We assume they're wrong, disrespectful, ignorant, or worse,deliberately offensive.

But what if… just maybe… they're operating from a **different narrative**?

Communication is Not Just About Words; It's About Worldviews

Every conversation is a collision of worldviews, and all collisions are bad.

We think we're just talking about who should lead the next project, or who left the dishes in the breakroom sink, or why someone didn't copy you on an email. But what we're really talking about are values, assumptions, and narratives that go unspoken but are heavily enforced.

- One person believes hierarchy should be respected. Another believes everyone should have an equal say.

- One person believes blunt honesty is efficient. Another believes diplomacy is respectful.

- One person believes lateness is inconsiderate. Another believes life happens, and grace is necessary.

Now, imagine these people on a Zoom call together. See the opportunities for tension? That's not poor communication. That's *unexamined narratives* crashing into each other at high speed.

Let's take a hypothetical workplace scenario.

Say you've got a team meeting. You, a team lead, are presenting a new initiative. Halfway through, a junior colleague interrupts and suggests a different approach, doing so publicly in front of the entire team. You feel heat rise in your chest.

Your internal dialogue goes something like this:

"Wow. That was incredibly disrespectful. Who do they think they are? I've been here ten years."

You leave the meeting frustrated and say to another manager later, "That employee has no respect for leadership. That team is out of control."

Now pause. Let's walk this back.

You believe they were disrespectful. But what's underneath that belief?

Probably something like:

"People should defer to leadership in public settings." "Good team members don't challenge authority in meetings." "There's a time and place for feedback."

That's your narrative. But what if their belief was:

"Ideas should be shared openly." "Good team members contribute in real time." "Collaboration means speaking up when it counts."

Same moment. Different narratives.

Now imagine if, instead of reacting, you reviewed and asked yourself,

"What narrative am I pulling from right now? Is this a personal standard, or a shared expectation?"

That one pause could turn a full-blown conflict into a deeper understanding, or even an opportunity to improve team culture.

When Beliefs Become Blind Spots

The real danger of deeply held beliefs isn't that they're wrong, it's that they're **invisible**. You don't recognize them as beliefs because you treat them as facts.

And that's exactly where communication starts to break down.

You assume your tone is appropriate, your feedback is helpful, your silence is respectful, and your transparency is empowering.

So when someone reacts with offense, frustration, or distance, you're confused. You think, "What's their problem?" Instead of asking, "What narrative are they operating from AND what narrative am I using in this scenario?"

Here's the tricky part: A belief that once **served you** can eventually **sabotage you**. What helped you succeed in one season can hold you back in the next, especially if you never stop to review whether it still fits the moment you're in.

Expired Beliefs: When the Facts Change

Remember my post-pregnancy jean story? I was standing in the mirror, wrestling with pants and denial at the same time. That moment wasn't just about clothes. It was about identity. It was about the story I'd been telling myself for nearly a decade:

"I'm a size 4. My clothes fit. That's just who I am."

But here's the reality: facts change.

Bodies change.

Seasons change.

Roles change.

Companies change.

Expectations change.

And yet our beliefs often get left behind at the change station. We cling to them like life rafts, even when the ocean has turned into a parking lot.

That's how you get:

- Managers who still believe the best way to build trust is to "keep work and personal separate", and then wonder why their teams feel disconnected, disengaged, and ready to quit.

- Parents trying to "fix" their grown children, convinced that they still need an "adult" to sign for them at the doctor's office, ignoring that their kid is 35 with a mortgage and a therapist.

- Voters clinging to a party line they inherited at the dinner table, never questioning if those policies still reflect their current values or lived reality.

- Entrepreneurs are convinced that hustle culture is the only path to success, burning out while trying to outwork a system that rewards visibility, not just effort.

The belief may have been true at one time. It may have been helpful. But is it now?

And more importantly, what happens when you carry that outdated narrative into your next conversation or conflict?

You misread tone, you assign intention, you defend before you understand, you talk past someone instead of to them.

All because your narrative is outdated.

Communication is a Mirror, Not a Microscope

Let's be honest: When communication goes sideways, most of us reach for the microscope. We zoom in on the other person's behavior like we're CSI agents at a crime scene.

"Why did they say it like that?"

"What's their problem?"

"Who raised them?"

But before you go full forensic investigator on someone's tone, try this instead: Hold up a mirror.

Instead of asking, "What's wrong with them?" ask, "What's informing me?"

This third step of DARE, **Review**, is the part where you stop assuming you're the baseline of normal and start examining the beliefs running your inner software.

Here are four questions to gut-check your communication defaults:

- What beliefs do I hold about how people should act, speak, present themselves, or behave?

- Where did those beliefs come from: family, culture, religion, reality TV?

- Are they still true, or just still familiar?

- Are they helping this moment… or making it harder?

This isn't easy work. It's mirror work, and mirror work is confronting, especially when what you see is outdated, inherited, or no longer helpful.

But here's why the work is worth it:

According to neuroscientists, your brain processes 11 million pieces of information per second, but you're only consciously aware of about 40.

That means most of your reactions aren't based on logic. They're based on legacy.

You're not responding to what's happening. Instead, you're responding to what you've *made it mean*, based on stories you absorbed a long time ago.

Let me give you an example.

Let's say you're from the U.S. and you're traveling abroad. You walk up to a small shop that looks like it might be closed, but a person is standing at the door. You make eye contact and ask,

"May I come in?"

They respond with a thumbs up.

You smile, take it as a yes, and start walking forward. Suddenly, the person's face changes. They look angry. They say something in a language you don't understand, but the tone? Oh, that's universal. And then you hear the part that cuts through:

"You Americans..."

So, what just happened?

Your narrative happened.

Your belief, the one you've never had to question, is that a thumbs up means:

"Yes."

"Go ahead."

"All good."

But in many cultures, a thumbs up isn't approval; it's an insult. It's the equivalent of flipping someone off.

So let me ask again: What happened?

You asked a question, and they gave you a gesture. Interpretively, you made that gesture mean "yes," because that's what it's always meant *to you*.

Now multiply that kind of misunderstanding by every email, meeting, marriage, group chat, and negotiation you've ever been in.

Can you see how easily narratives collide, especially when they've never been examined?

And the more unexamined those narratives are, the more rigid your communication becomes.

You don't listen to understand, you listen to defend the script you didn't even realize you were following. You think you're being clear, but really, you're being consistent with your old programming.

But when you review, *honestly review*, you start to hold your beliefs more open-handedly.

You create room for nuance. For change. For growth.

You start saying things like:

"This is what I've believed… but I'm open to learning something new."

That's real leadership. That's adulting at a higher level.

Now, let's take a little detour so we can get back to what we're talking about.

My narrative suggests that some of you read the last section and immediately crossed your arms. My narrative is so vivid, I can see someone right now, arms crossed, lips poked out, chest getting tight as you feel confronted by **Review**,

"So you're telling me everything I believe is wrong? Toss it all out and become a blank slate?"

If that's you, hold tight. I get it. "That's not what I said" (see what I did there). We will walk through this together.

What I *am* saying is this: There are some old, outdated narratives you're carrying that are not serving you anymore. And in some cases, they're doing real harm.

Those are the beliefs I want you to question. Those are the ones I want you to put on the table, hold up to the light, and ask: "Is this helping me, or holding me back?"

What Happens When You Don't Review

Let's not sugarcoat it, unreviewed narratives are the breeding ground for some of the messiest workplace and relationship drama.

They're behind:

- Emails that say "per my last message" (a.k.a. corporate shade)

- Comments that start with "No offense, but…" (spoiler: offense is coming)

- Managers who confuse control with leadership

- Unchecked assumptions based on someone's name, age, gender, skin tone, or schooling

- Broken policies no one questions because "we've always done it this way."

- And worst of all… they keep us stuck.

You cannot grow a relationship, shift a team dynamic, or reinvent yourself while running on beliefs that haven't been updated since the days of dial-up internet.

Better Beliefs = Better Conversations

This isn't about deleting your whole system of values. It's about **editing**, cleaning out the junk drawer of outdated beliefs, and upgrading the ones worth keeping.

Let's make it plain:

- Maybe you were taught that *speaking up is disrespectful.* But now you're a leader, and silence reads as disengagement.

- Maybe you believed that *staying late proves you care.* But you're building a team that prioritizes balance, not burnout.

118

- Maybe you've internalized the idea that *you have to be twice as good to get half as far.*

But now you're exhausted from performing for people who already benefit from your brilliance.

Time to review and update:

When you revise your beliefs, you revise the quality of your relationships.

You create space for empathy, clarity, and genuine connection.

The Worst Narrative

We can't discuss reviewing beliefs without addressing one of the most damaging types of narratives: the stories we tell ourselves about other people.

These are the assumptions we make based on factors such as race, ethnicity, gender, age, job title, education level, or plain stereotypes. They're often unspoken, but they're loud in impact.

These narratives influence everything, including who gets hired, who gets heard, who gets promoted, and who gets dismissed. They seep into how we vote, how we parent, how we lead, and how we communicate. At their most extreme, they lead to injustice, bad policy, and even war. But more often, they show up in ways that feel small, until they're not.

When they show up at work, we say things like:

- "They're from marketing, they don't get operations."
- "Finance people don't care about people, only numbers."
- "They're in HR, they're always going to take the company's side."
- "They're new, what do they really know?"

Even if we never say these things out loud, we bring them into the room.

And here's the problem: **If I approach a conversation already believing something about you, I'm not showing up to connect or understand. I'm showing up to confirm.**

119

That's not a conversation. That's a script with a predictable ending.

Let me tell you a real-life story that brings this to life.

I walked into an executive-level client meeting, where I was the executive and strategist, hired to guide a multi-million-dollar organizational transformation. I walked in confidently, greeted the group, and said:

> "Is everyone ready to get the meeting started?"

Before anyone else could speak, one person looked up, smiled politely, and said:

> "Shouldn't we wait for the person in charge to arrive?"

I paused, more amused than offended, and asked:

> "Who exactly should we be waiting for?"

And without hesitation, they said:

> "We should wait for *him* to arrive."

That's when I laughed and said:

> "Well, *he* is a *her,* and *her* is *me.* I think all parties are present, so let's get started."

Now let's be clear: I didn't walk into the room appearing shy or unsure. I didn't look confused.

The only reason they didn't believe I was the person in charge was because of their narrative — one that said the "executive" was going to be a man. The person who said it turned beet red, apologized, and appeared to be mortified. It did not change that his narrative showed up and got the meeting off to a very awkward start. (If you are saying, "Dethra, we don't know what he was thinking or why he assumed the leader would be a man, let me put your mind at ease. He later apologized and admitted that his narrative got in the way.)

That's what happens when narratives go unreviewed. You misread the moment, and in doing so, you undermine your ability to engage meaningfully.

But, let's be honest, **we all have a "them."**

You know exactly what I mean. *There* might be a type of person, a group, a generation, a race, a department, a political party, a pronoun, or a zip code. And how did you get your "them"? Oh, it's easy.

Some of us inherited "them." They came gift-wrapped from our families or communities, passed down at the dinner table like cornbread and commentary.

Others were shaped by one negative experience that got blown up into a life philosophy:

"I worked with *them* once... never again." "You know how *they* are."

Some of us were spoon-fed narratives through media, TV, film, and news cycles that highlight the worst examples and broadcast them as the rule, not the exception.

And here's the kicker: we don't always notice it, but our bodies do. We shift in our seats, our tone tightens, our trust drops 10 degrees. We assume intentions, we offer fewer chances, and worst of all? We communicate to confirm our narrative, not challenge it.

That's how bias operates: quietly, efficiently, repeatedly.

So, what do we do about it?

First, we **admit** we've got a "them." Then we **listen** to the story we tell ourselves when someone from that group speaks up, takes charge, makes a mistake, or simply walks into the room. Next, we **interrupt** that story before it becomes action. Finally, we **retrain** the narrative with truth, not just what we've heard, but what we've chosen to learn and unlearn.

Because let's be honest: the worst narratives aren't just the ones that limit *your* potential, they're the ones that block your ability to see *other people's* brilliance, value, and capacity.

You can't build trust, lead a team, or have a real conversation while holding someone hostage to a story they had no part in, and you never questioned.

So yes, review the narratives you've accepted about yourself. But don't stop there. Review the ones you've built about *them* too.

That's where the real work and real connection begins.

The Real Invitation

The "R" in DARE is your invitation to interrupt the autopilot. To stop mid-thought, mid-sentence, even mid-eye-roll, and ask:

"What belief am I acting from right now?" "Do I still want to believe that?"

Because not everything you believe is wrong, but *everything* you believe deserves a review. And the better you get at reviewing your narratives, the better you become at navigating conflict, building trust, and showing up as the version of you that isn't just reacting, but leading.

Now let's look at what happens when someone doesn't review and how that plays out in the wild world of work.

Why "Working Hard" Isn't Always Enough for Career Success

Let's talk about a narrative that's baked into every motivational poster, every commencement speech, and every "how to get ahead" career panel on LinkedIn:

"If you work hard, you'll be rewarded."

It sounds right. It feels noble. And for a while, it works.

Until it doesn't.

Meet Janelle.

Janelle is smart, sharp, and ambitious. First-generation college grad. Black woman. Corporate strategist. She's the kind of employee companies love to highlight in their annual report and forget in their day-to-day pipeline planning. But she didn't know that. At least not at first.

When she started her job, she bought the narrative wholesale: put your head down, do the work, and eventually someone will notice.

And so she worked. Hard. Late nights, skipped lunches, volunteered for the messy projects no one wanted. She got feedback like "reliable," "solid," and "dependable." At first, those words felt like gold stars.

Then she noticed she wasn't climbing the ladder the way she thought; in other words, her advancement wasn't in correlation to her efforts. So, what did she do? She worked harder.

And, lifted her head just enough to start taking notice of the office around her.

She noticed the guy down the hall who always left at five but somehow got tapped for the innovation task force.

She noticed the bubbly coworker who stumbled through presentations but was always invited into big meetings.

She noticed the junior analyst who got promoted to manager after six months, while she had been waiting for her name to come up in "the right conversation" for three years.

And slowly, the narrative she had clung to — just work hard and when that doesn't work, work harder — started to unravel.

The Frustration of Following the Script

The worst part wasn't that others were advancing. It was that the rules she was told to follow didn't apply to everyone.

That's when the frustration set in.

"Why do I have to prove myself ten times over?" "Why is my value only measured in output, while theirs is measured in visibility?" "Why am I waiting for my boss to advocate for me like a fairy godparent?"

The questions were layered, but the **layers were really in the narratives driving the questions.**

It wasn't until she asked a trusted mentor why she kept getting overlooked that the truth came out—she wasn't seen as a leader because no one knew she wanted to be one. She wasn't self-promoting; some saw her lack of self-promotion as a lack of ambition, while others viewed it as contentment in her current role. Her quiet confidence wasn't perceived as power; rather, it was misread as passivity.

She worked in operations, and many leaders in the organization viewed operations as a department full of "doers," not "leaders", not the kind of people you tap to lead cross-functional initiatives or manage large teams.

And the biggest problem of all? Janelle believed that hard work alone should be enough.

But here's the thing about unreviewed narratives: they will eventually betray you.

And here's the twist: most of us don't realize the narrative is malfunctioning, because it doesn't always break like a dropped plate. It breaks like a disagreement, a moment of frustration, a deep sense of being overlooked, an argument where you're certain they're wrong, a performance review that feels unfair, a promotion that goes to someone else, and your gut reaction is *"How did that happen?"* or worse, *"That should've been me."*

That's how unreviewed narratives show up when they're crumbling: not as blatant affronts, but as invisible tension. You don't think, *"Maybe my story's outdated."* You think, *"They don't see me. They don't value me. Something is broken out there."*

But sometimes, what's broken isn't just out there. It's the story you've been using to make sense of your success, and until you review it, you'll keep reacting to the symptoms instead of addressing the source.

When Narratives Stop Working, We Have Two Options: Remain or Review

When the story we've been living by stops working, we are constantly faced with a choice:

Remain or Review.

Remaining feels easier at first. Familiar. Comfortable, even. It's the story we already know, the one we've been told by mentors, reinforced by our families, modeled by people we trusted, and confirmed by a few early wins. The story says, *"This is how the world works,"* and even when that story starts to betray us, we cling to it. We tell ourselves the rules just need more time to kick in. Or, that others, the people not doing it our way, are breaking the rules.

When we remain, we double down. We convince ourselves that the problem must be *them*, the coworkers, the leaders, the system. We say things like:

"People just don't appreciate hard work anymore.""Leadership is playing favorites." "These younger folks don't have to put in what I did." "They must be cutting corners. That's why they're moving up."

And suddenly, the frustration that should've led us to **review** becomes fuel to **entrench.** Instead of examining and changing the narrative, we fight to defend it, even if it's no longer (or never was) true.

That's what nearly happened to Janelle.

After years of loyalty, she reached a breaking point. The promotion she believed she had earned went to someone else again, and the voice in her head got loud:

"This place is rigged." "People like me don't get promoted." "What's the point of trying?"

She had a choice. She could remain in that story, where she worked hard, stayed overlooked, and silently resented everyone else who seemed to be playing a different game. Or she could **review.** And to review meant doing something uncomfortable: it meant admitting that her story, though once useful, was no longer serving her.

It meant letting go of her identity as the "hardest worker in the room" and asking, *"What does success actually require here?"* It meant replacing disappointment with strategy. Reviewing isn't about blaming yourself. It's about **reclaiming your power.**

Janelle realized she wasn't stuck because she lacked talent. She was stuck because she was playing chess on a checkerboard, following rules that did not fit the game she was in.

So she did the unthinkable: she stopped grinding, started watching, studying, and strategizing.

She built relationships, made herself visible, not just valuable, stopped aligning with the hustle, and started aligning with power.

And then?

She LEFT!

She walked away from the organization that put more emphasis on visibility than productivity. She stepped into a space where her contribution was valued, her presence was respected, and the leadership actually walked the talk.

Now, be honest, did Janelle's leaving the organization catch you off guard?

Were you rooting for the "and then she got promoted!" ending?

It's okay. That's the narrative we've been taught to expect. But that's not how the **DARE model** works, and that's *definitely* not what **Review** is about.

Review isn't a magic trick. It's not "fix your mindset, get your trophy." It's the bold, often uncomfortable act of asking:

> Is this story I'm living by still true? Was it ever true? Does it still work for me? And, does it work here?

Sometimes the answer is:

> "This narrative was never mine."

Other times:

> "It might work somewhere else, but not here."

And when that happens, you've got two choices: Change the story or change the setting.

Because sometimes remaining means staying in the narrative or the room.

Both will cost you.

The remaining feels righteous, like you're being loyal to the grind. Reviewing feels risky, like you're stepping off the map. But let me be clear: only one of them will get you where you're meant to be.

You always have a choice: stay stuck in the narrative or start to create a new one.

So What Does "Review" Look Like in a Conversation?

Janelle's story was a career example, but the real lesson here isn't just about work. It's about how we show up in every conversation. In the same way we carry outdated narratives into our jobs, we also bring them into our interactions with people.

We think we're just talking about a deadline, a decision, or a disagreement, but really, we're dragging in assumptions about who's right, who gets to lead, who's allowed to speak up, who should stay in their lane, what "professional" looks like, and what respect sounds like.

And that's why Review matters.

The "R" in DARE isn't just about self-reflection in private; it's about self-awareness in real time. It's the pause that saves the conversation. It's the inner dialogue that says:

"Wait, what am I assuming here?" "What belief is fueling my tone, my response, my silence, my defensiveness?" "Do I know what they meant, or am I reacting to my narrative?"

That's conversational competence. It's not just speaking clearly, it's listening with curiosity. It's noticing the story behind the reaction. It's recognizing that what you believe is happening in a conversation may not be what's happening.

Review doesn't always change the outcome of a conversation. But it will change your approach to it. It will help you:

- Challenge the knee-jerk reactions you've mistaken for instincts
- Stay present instead of defensive
- Ask better questions
- Resist rushing to judgment
- Create space for clarity, not just closure

The power of Review is that it creates space, and in that space, connection becomes possible. Because every difficult conversation is shaped by what you believe to be true.

And until you review those beliefs, you'll always risk responding to the story in your head, rather than the person and conversation in front of you.

How to Review in Real Time: Spot the Narrative, Save the Conversation

Let's bring it home.

Everything we've explored in this chapter, about Janelle, the workplace, assumptions, and frustration, it all boil down to this:

Narratives run the show, and until you review those narratives, they'll continue to hijack your conversations and call it communication.

So, how do you use Review in real time? What does it look like in a heated meeting, a tense one-on-one, or that awkward family dinner where someone says the thing and your brain gives the signal to lose it?

Let's break it down. Here's how to Review mid-conversation while staying engaged and not sounding robotic.

Step 1: Recognize When a Narrative Is at Play

You'll know a narrative is taking over when your internal monologue starts speaking louder than the actual person in front of you.

If your brain is shouting things like:

"They don't respect me." "Those people always..."

Pause. That's not the conversation, that's the *story* you're telling about the conversation.

Narratives get loud when we feel uncertain, disrespected, or emotionally exposed. So, when your reaction spikes, ask yourself:

"What's the story I just started telling myself?"

Now you're in Review.

Step 2: Walk Yourself Back

Once you've spotted the story, the goal isn't to shut it down; it's to slow it down. Instead of reacting to your narrative, say (internally or aloud):

"Let me pause for a second. I might be filling in gaps with old stories."

This isn't you backing down. It's you backing up to get the full picture.

Neuroscience tells us that when we pause to reflect before reacting, we engage our prefrontal cortex, the part of the brain responsible for decision-making. Translation: less fight-or-flight, more strategy and self-control.

Step 3: Assess the Accuracy of Your Narrative

Now comes the real work: ask yourself three simple questions:

1. Was this true?
2. Is this still true?
3. Is this helping me have a better conversation?

This is where Review becomes powerful. You're not just checking your facts, you're checking your framing.

Sometimes the narrative is outdated. Sometimes it's based on one experience you turned into a rule, and sometimes it's not wrong, but it's not helpful right now.

And that's what you're after, helpful, not just accurate.

Step 4: Invite the Other Person to Review (Without Sounding Like a Therapist)

Now, here's the magic trick. You can get someone else to reflect on *their* narrative without ever using the word "narrative."

Try saying:

"I want to make sure I'm not bringing in baggage from another conversation. Can we walk through what just happened together?"

"Can I share the story that popped into my head, and you tell me if I'm off?"
"I might be interpreting this through my lens. What were you trying to communicate?"

These are Review prompts. They invite the other person to examine what they meant, what they assumed, and how it landed, all without defensiveness.

According to Harvard Business Review, when we create space for mutual reflection, conversations become more productive, less reactive, and more likely to end in resolution.

Step 5: Return to the Shared Goal

Review isn't just about clarity, it's about *progress*. So once both of you have had a chance to reflect and reframe, bring the conversation back to purpose:

"Okay, now that we've cleared that up, what do we want to walk away with?"
"How do we move forward from here in a way that works for both of us?"

This shifts the conversation from confusion to collaboration.

Because that's the goal of conversational competence. Not to win. Not to vent. But to connect and move forward.

Final Word: Review Is the Turning Point

Of all the steps in the DARE model, Review is the one that transforms a conversation from explosive to effective. It turns reaction into reflection, assumption into awareness, and disagreement into a doorway, not a dead end.

So the next time you feel yourself getting frustrated, defensive, or ready to shut down, stop and ask:

"What narrative just showed up in the room?"

Then: "Was it true, is it still true, and is it helping me?"

That one pause, that one internal Review, might be all it takes to turn a trainwreck of a conversation into a breakthrough.

You don't need to fix everything; you just need to be willing to review what's driving you because when you review your story, you can rewrite the ending.

And that's where conversational competence begins.

Chapter 5 Recap: Review the Narrative(s) You Have Accepted as Fact

Cliff Notes, Dethra-Style:

You're not crazy, you're just reacting to a story you didn't realize you were telling yourself. Whether it's about a pair of jeans, a missed promotion, or a coworker's tone, your brain is always working off a script. The problem? You didn't write most of it.

This chapter? It's about holding that script up to the light and asking:

"Wait… did I choose this? Or just inherit it with the family china?"

Key Takeaways:

- Most of what you believe is inherited, not investigated.

- Narratives shape your reactions long before facts have a chance to take effect.

- Beliefs that once helped you can now be sabotaging your communication.

- The worst narratives are often the ones we believe about *other people*.

- Review is about truth, timing, and whether that story still works for *you* and *the moment.*

In a conversation, Review means pausing to ask:

"Is this narrative helping… or hijacking?"

Why This Matters:

Unreviewed narratives are the root of most miscommunication. At work, they lead to conflict, missed promotions, and toxic team dynamics.

In relationships, they fuel resentment, silence, or full-on blowups over nothing.

In leadership, they make you blind to talent, resistance, or truth. And, in a conflict, they lead to the parties butting heads and getting stuck.

131

Review is the moment where you choose clarity over comfort, and that's where real connection begins.

Call to Action:

Next time a conversation triggers you, pause. Ask yourself:

- What's the story I'm telling myself right now?

- Was it true?

- Is it still true?

- Is it helping or hurting this moment?

- Then, instead of reacting to the narrative, respond with curiosity.

That's how you build conversational competence: one internal Review at a time.

Chapter 6

Engage for Conversation,
Not Conversion

The Story: The Wedding That Almost Had a Walkout

It started with a simple toast.

We were at my friend's wedding— intimate and beautifully chaotic like most family events. People were halfway into their third or fourth glasses of champagne when the groom's uncle stood up, tapped his glass, and started what we thought would be a charming speech. By the sound of his voice, we knew he was a little bit tipsy and that this was going to be *good*.

But we had no idea what was coming.

Out of nowhere, he put his hand on his wife's shoulder and said, "You know, marriage only works when the woman knows her place."

As I clutched the pearls I didn't even have on, I scanned the room and knew things were about to get spicy. I also immediately pulled out my phone to take notes because I knew this was going to end up in the book.

You could *feel* the air shift. Forks froze mid-bite. The bride's aunt whispered, "Jesus, be a fence." Another whispered back, "Be a muzzle."

Two tables away, the bride's sister—Harvard Law, feminist, and freshly promoted to partner—stood up and yelled, "If Jesus existed, his momma would've had an abortion instead of having him."

And just like that, the whole room erupted into chaos.

Everyone was so busy trying to be heard that they lost sight of the actual point.

And what was the point?

No, seriously—pause for a second and answer that question. What was the point?

Because it wasn't about gender roles or theology or who had the best rebuttal or the strongest argument.

The point was the *wedding*. The *moment*. The couple at the center of it all.

But no one could hear the person saying, "STOP! You're ruining their day."

That's what happens when we skip the "E" in DARE.

Engage is not about overpowering. It's not about winning. It's not about changing someone's mind so you can high-five yourself for being right.

Engage means participating in the actual conversation, not hijacking it. It's the moment you take all the internal work of DARE (Describe, Acknowledge, Review)… and let it guide how you speak. It's where the model moves from mindset to mouth.

When you Engage, the goal is not conversion; it's *connection*. It's listening, responding, and contributing in a way that moves the dialogue forward, rather than setting it on fire.

When people fight to be heard but forget *why* they're talking in the first place, they fall into the conversion trap. They stop seeking understanding and start chasing control. And that's how you ruin the moment, whether it's a wedding, a workplace, or a one-on-one conversation that could've changed everything.

Why "Winning" an Argument Is the Worst Possible Goal

Let's start with the truth: some people are so obsessed with being "right" that they will burn down the conversation just to stand in the ashes yelling, *"Told you so."*

If I'm being honest, I used to be that person.

I was raised on logic, trained in strategy, and fluent in receipts. My brain moves fast. My words move even faster. And for a long time, that meant I was good at debate, great at presentations, and terrible at any conversation that wasn't about winning. If there was no score to settle or point to prove, I didn't know what to do. So I made every conversation a competition because someone had to lose, and it wasn't going to be me.

Here's what I've learned: *you can win the argument and still lose the opportunity*, which means you can be "right" yet still be completely ineffective.

Let's break that down.

The Illusion of Victory

Winning a conversation feels good. There's a surge of pride, a hit of validation, and a brief moment where you feel powerful, like you've proven your point and walked away with the crown that no one knew existed.

But here's the catch: that kind of win usually costs more than it's worth.

When someone tries to "win" an argument, what they're doing is clinging to their **position**, not focusing on the underlying **interest**—and that's where conversations go sideways.

Let's pause here for a second and unpack these two terms, which are foundational in the world of conflict resolution and mediation—specifically in **ADR**, or **Alternative Dispute Resolution**.

I'm going to oversimplify this to make it easy to apply:

- A **position** is *what* someone says they want.

- An **interest** is *why* they want it.

This distinction is critical. Because while positions often clash, **interests usually overlap**.

Take this common example from education:

- Teachers may demand higher salaries.

- School boards may push for increased performance standards. At first glance, it sounds like opposing sides. But when you peel back the positions, both groups share a common interest: **better outcomes for students**.

But how do people end up in opposing positions if their interests actually overlap?

Because each party—the "individual parties," as they're called in dispute resolution—believes that *their "what" is the only way to achieve the "why,"* and when they don't truly engage in conversation, they get so locked into their *"what"* that they lose sight of the *"why"* altogether.

Let's go back to the teacher and school board example.

According to USA Today, **over** 90% of teachers spend their own money on classroom supplies each year, with the average out-of-pocket cost hovering around **$750.** From the teacher's perspective, a pay increase feels urgent and justified because they're funding the school system with their bank accounts. But too often, the debate stops at "We need higher pay," instead of fully explaining the *why*:

To properly educate our students, we need access to supplies that aren't currently funded by the school system. As it stands, our salaries aren't enough to support our families and provide our students with the necessary materials for a quality education. So if we're expected to personally subsidize a system that's supposed to be publicly funded, we need to be paid accordingly, so our students don't suffer.

On the other side, school boards often fixate on performance standards. But according to the same USA Today report, 45% of public schools are understaffed, and that number jumps to 57% in high-poverty districts. While they're pushing for higher outcomes, they may be ignoring the systemic strain that makes achieving those outcomes harder.

Here's what's happening:

- Teachers are thinking, *"If you pay me more, I can afford the tools and resources my students need to succeed."*

- School boards are thinking, *"If we raise expectations, teachers will step up and student outcomes will improve."*

Both parties are chasing the *same interest*—better education and improved student outcomes—but their commitment to *their position* keeps them in conflict.

Because they won't engage. Because they're stuck in the "how" instead of aligning on the "why."

Engagement is what opens that door. It shifts the focus away from entrenched positions and back toward shared interests. And *that* is where real problem-solving happens, not in the win, but in the work.

But when someone is obsessed with winning, they get stuck defending their position like it's a hill to die on.

And once the conversation becomes about who's right instead of what's right—or even why we're here—it's no longer collaboration, it's competition."

This isn't just theory, it's backed by decades of negotiation research. The Harvard Negotiation Project, one of the leading voices in conflict resolution, emphasizes this very shift: focusing on interests rather than positions leads to more durable, creative, and mutually beneficial outcomes.

So the next time you feel yourself digging in to "win," ask yourself: Am I defending a position or serving a shared interest?

In real life, especially in workplaces, families, and partnerships, there's usually more at stake than just being right. You have to maintain trust, preserve respect, and protect the ability to work together tomorrow.

What's the point of "winning" if the person on the other end is too hurt, shut down, or embarrassed to talk to you again?

There's another powerful reason to engage for **conversation**, not **conversion**.

Think back to a time when you were deep in an argument, a debate you were *sure* you were winning. You had the proof, your logic was solid and you were two moves away from metaphorically yelling *"Checkmate!"*

You felt like a strategic genius.

And then... It happened.

That horrible, humbling shift: a new piece of information dropped into the conversation, and suddenly, the tables turned. What you thought was an airtight and indisputable fact simply was not, and worst of all –brace yourself– you were *wrong*.

Now what?

What do you do when the mic you were about to drop boomerangs back and hits you in the mouth?

I did a small survey of 675 people and asked them this exact question. Over 96% admitted to sticking to their original position even *after* they had been proven wrong, because they couldn't bear the hit to their ego after being so adamant.

What's even more alarming? More than half of those who admitted they had stayed the course after realizing they were wrong also said they *still* won the argument.

Let that sink in: they were wrong, they knew they were wrong, but they won because they refused to back down once they had already defended their position so fiercely.

The longer you cling to a position, the harder it becomes to care about the interest. The more you focus on winning or *being right*, the less room you have to *do what's right.*

Engage keeps you from locking in too early. It gives you space to stay in dialogue, to explore the real issue, and to gather the data you need to take a position that's aligned with the bigger goal.

Let me be clear, this is *not* a "stand for nothing, fall for anything" doctrine. This is a "hear and be heard" guide to conversational competence. This is about staying curious long enough to take a stand that serves the outcome, not just your ego.

The Workplace Wrecking Ball

Let's bring it into the office.

Imagine two coworkers—Tina and Brandon—leading a project with high visibility. During a meeting, they disagree on the direction of a campaign. Tina has more data; Brandon has more experience. The conversation turns tense, and Brandon, determined to "win," begins cutting Tina off, rolling his eyes, and referencing his track record of past successes. Eventually, Tina goes silent. Leadership sides with Brandon, and his idea moves forward.

From the outside, Brandon won. But inside the team, things just broke.

Tina is now disengaged. Others on the team, who witnessed how Tina was treated, no longer feel safe contributing bold ideas. The manager begins to receive feedback about "tension" within the team. The nail in the coffin was when the next project rolled around: it was a high-stakes initiative with a lot of visibility, and under normal circumstances, people would have jumped at the opportunity to be on the project. It was announced that Brandon would lead the project, and people began withdrawing their names from consideration for the project. Word got around, and no one wanted to work with Brandon.

He won the argument but lost his reputation.

In the workplace, "winners" like Brandon often become isolated leaders. People stop bringing them problems. They get left off early brainstorming invites, they hear the phrase "We just didn't think you'd be interested" more than they hear "What do you think?"

Because no one wants to work with someone who always has to win.

Why We Do It (Even When We Know Better)

Let's be clear: the urge to win is human. It's wrapped up in ego, identity, and sometimes even survival. If you grew up in environments where being wrong meant being punished, dismissed, or unheard, then being right becomes armor.

But in mature, healthy communication, being right isn't the goal; being effective is.

When we prioritize winning:

- We interrupt instead of inquire.

- We assume instead of ask.

- We listen for weakness, not for wisdom.

Even worse, we start to talk *at* people instead of *with* them. And the conversation becomes a monologue for the audience instead of a dialogue.

When I Had to Check Myself

This isn't theory for me. It's lived experience.

There was a time in my professional life when I was known as *the person with the answers*. If you wanted the best strategy, the cleanest plan, the most airtight rationale—call Dethra.

But if you wanted to talk it through or needed space to process your ideas without being corrected or outpaced? Get someone else to do it. Everyone knew it except for me.

And when I realized that… it stung.

That realization hit one day as I walked past a group of "friends" huddled in a conference room. They were scribbling ideas on the whiteboard, surrounded by pizza boxes, Coca-Cola, sweet tea, and the kind of laughter that makes you peek in just to see what's so funny.

I popped my head in. "What's up?"

Suddenly, silence. Everyone froze like I had just walked in on them plotting a bank heist. Eyes darted around the room, clearly waiting for someone to be brave enough to answer. Finally, Chevy spoke up:

"Well, Dethra, we're working on a project."

A project? We were on the same team. What project?

Another person jumped in, trying to help Chevy out. "Well, it's a new project, not ready for a bunch of people to be involved just yet."

A bunch? I thought. There are already five of you here.

Then came the gut punch from the one person I considered a real friend, not just a colleague.

She looked at me and said, "Girl, no one felt like being argued down by you today."

She kept going.

"This is a brainstorming session. There's no right or wrong, nothing has to make sense yet. We're just throwing stuff at the wall, laughing through it, and seeing what sticks. No pressure. That's *not* what you're good at.

Now, when we have a solid idea and are ready for strategy and an execution plan, you'll be the first person we call. Because no one in the world does that better than you."

And she was right.

I always had my data together. I was sharp. Beating me in a debate was practically impossible. I had built a reputation as the woman with the answers.

I was winning!

But I was also building a brand as someone who cared more about being *right* than being *relational.*

And that's not who I wanted to be: that's not the kind of leader I wanted to be. But, I wasn't just that way at work, and it made me realize that's not the kind of daughter, partner, or coach I wanted to be either.

So I had to learn to listen differently, to slow down, to stop waiting for my turn to speak and instead focus on understanding, to ask myself, mid-conversation:

- Do I understand the point the other person is trying to make?

- Have I considered how valid their point is before defending mine?

- Could I honestly summarize their perspective—without sarcasm or finding holes in their logic—right now?

If the answer was "no," then I wasn't engaging. I was positioning, performing, and powering up for a win.

Engagement Is Not Surrender

Let's be real. Sometimes people equate listening with weakness. They think, "If I don't argue back, they'll think they're right." "If I don't assert my side, I'll get walked over." "If I don't fight for my point, I lose."

But here's what's true: engaging is not surrender, it's strategy.

When you listen well, when you ask questions that clarify instead of condemn, when you reflect what you heard before presenting your view, you don't lose power, you gain it.

You show emotional intelligence, you build relational capital, you become someone people trust because they know you're not just waiting for your next rebuttal.

And when you finally do share your point? People *hear* it because you've modeled what it means to engage instead of dominate.

What to Aim for Instead

Instead of "winning," aim for:

- **Clarity** – Are we talking about the real issue, or are we spiraling around a distraction?

- **Connection** – Do we understand where the other person is coming from, even if we disagree?

- **Collaboration** – Can we find a path forward that honors more than one perspective while achieving our shared interest?

- **Continuity** – Will this conversation set us up to work or relate better in the future?

The truth is, most meaningful conversations don't end with "You're right." They end with, *"That makes sense." "I hadn't thought of it like that." "Let's keep talking."*

That's engagement. That's growth. And that's what DARE is designed to help you do.

The Difference Between Listening to Understand versus Listening to Respond

I've mentioned "listening to respond" more than a few times. Let's talk about what it means, what it looks like in action, and the impact it can have on a conversation.

We've all been there. Someone's talking, and we're *technically* listening, but we're not *hearing* them. We're scanning for flaws in their logic, silently crafting the perfect comeback, or waiting for them to take a breath so we can finally say what we've been thinking since minute one.

That's not listening: That's reloading.

The truth is, many of us have mastered the art of pretending to listen while mentally preparing to respond. We nod at the right time, throw in a well-placed 'mmhmm,' maybe even ask a question that sounds thoughtful. Sometimes, it's not just about winning the point—it's about managing social anxiety and appearing engaged. But the preoccupation with appearing engaged can distract us from actually being engaged. The preoccupations mean our real goal isn't understanding, it's convincing. It's landing our point. It's winning.

And that's the problem.

Listening to understand and listening to respond are not the same. They aren't even distant cousins. They are fundamentally different ways of engaging. One builds bridges. The other builds walls. One is an olive branch, and one is a gauntlet.

Listening to respond means you already have your conclusion in mind. Your mind is closed, and you're simply waiting for your turn to speak. But you're not in the conversation to *hear*. You're there to have your say and *win*.

Listening to understand is something else entirely. It's a slower, more deliberate process. It's rooted in curiosity, not responding, not looking good or saving face, not combat. It's when you're open to the idea that your perspective might shift—or at the very least, expand.

It doesn't mean you don't have an opinion. It just means you're willing to form that opinion responsibly, with all the information, not just the parts you like.

Let's put that difference into action.

Meet Jamal. He's sharp, analytical, and respected at his company. When a colleague, Priya, challenges his proposal during a planning meeting, Jamal does what many competent, seasoned professionals do: he braces. Internally, he thinks, "She misunderstood. I've got this." His body tenses. His mind starts preparing his counterpoints. The room hasn't shifted, but his posture has. He's no longer collaborating. He's defending.

As Priya continues, she begins to lay out her concerns and questions that could refine the proposal, not criticisms. But Jamal isn't present anymore. He's listening just enough to find the flaw in her thinking. And when he speaks, it's confident, composed, and completely dismissive.

The team falls quiet. Priya withdraws. And Jamal, who "won" the disagreement, walks out feeling like he handled it well.

Except he didn't.

Later, his manager pulls him aside. "You're brilliant, Jamal, but you bulldozed the room today. You had a chance to make that a better idea—with help—and instead you shut it down."

And just like that, he "won" the debate but lost sight of the goal.

This is what happens when we mistake performance for participation, when we confuse being right with being relational, when we skip *engagement* and go straight to rebuttal.

Let me tell you something uncomfortable: people who always have to be right rarely get the best out of others. Because when people don't feel heard, they stop contributing. They start playing it safe. They hold back ideas. And in the long run, that doesn't just hurt feelings, it hurts innovation, growth, and results.

The research is clear. According to a study published in the *Harvard Business Review*, employees who feel heard are more engaged, more motivated, and more loyal. Teams led by leaders who practice active listening are significantly more likely to hit performance targets and report higher levels of psychological safety. Listening—real listening—isn't just a soft skill, it's a competitive advantage.

But it's not easy. Especially when you're used to being the most intelligent person in the room.

I get it. I've lived it.

There was a time when I could feel myself gearing up to respond before the other person even finished their sentence. I already knew what they were trying to say, and I was ready to fix it, clarify it, or counter it.

And it wasn't because I didn't care. I *did* care. But I thought that listening meant *solving*. That understanding meant *explaining back*. That being a good communicator meant being quick, clear, and conclusive. What I didn't realize was that my speed made people feel steamrolled. My "clarity" sometimes made them feel erased. And my confidence could sound like control.

I wasn't trying to dominate, I was trying to help. But I was doing it from a place of assumption, not attention.

I had to learn a new rule: **Shut up.**

I spent a long time trying to turn Shut Up into an acronym—something soft, clever, professional-sounding. But I couldn't. Let me be

honest: I *decided* not to because some truths don't need softening. This is one of them.

If you want to get to the heart of the issue, if you genuinely want to listen to understand, you have to stop filling the space with your words. You have to give other people's ideas and voices room to breathe.

Let me give you a tool I started using, and now I teach it to my clients who are rapid idea generators (that is what I call us): the 5-second rule.

Before you respond, pause for five seconds. Before you ask a question, wait for five seconds.

It's simple, but it's not easy. That 5-second silence feels long. But in those seconds, something powerful happens: your brain stops reacting and starts reflecting. You remember that this isn't a race, it's a conversation.

And in that pause, you give the other person something rare: the gift of not being rushed.

It sounds like:

- "Tell me more about what you're seeing."

- "What information are you working with?"

- "Help me understand what matters most to you right now."

And if the energy feels tense or competitive, I've learned to call it out directly yet respectfully.

- "It feels like we're rushing to solve without really hearing each other. Can we slow this down?"

- "We both have strong opinions here. Are you open to hearing mine after I fully understand yours?"

These kinds of statements change the conversation; they shift the room. Because they signal maturity, they signal trust, and they signal that you're not here to convert, you're here to *connect*.

Let's be honest: most people don't know the difference between hearing and listening.

They think because they *heard* the words, they listened, but real listening is active, intentional, and generous.

It means showing up with the kind of presence that says, "Your perspective matters. Even if I disagree, I respect your thought process. And I'm not going to bulldoze my way to being right."

People love leaders who listen, not just because it feels good, but because it *works*. Teams thrive when they know their input isn't being filtered through a leader's agenda, but through a leader's curiosity.

They feel safer sharing bold ideas. They feel more comfortable admitting mistakes early. They become more invested in collective success.

And all of that? It starts with the difference between listening to respond and listening to understand.

So here's the challenge for you, one I still give to myself:

In your next conversation, ask yourself:

- "Am I listening to build—or to win?"
- "Do I truly understand their point, or am I just waiting for them to finish talking?"
- "Could I honestly summarize their perspective before offering mine?"

And if the answer is no, then pause. Listen again because that pause might be the most powerful thing you bring to the conversation.

That pause is where empathy lives, where ideas grow, and where engagement begins.

And that's what "E" in DARE is all about—not just talking, but *transforming* how we talk. Not just being heard, but truly hearing.

Because when we listen to understand, we don't just resolve conflict—we build relationships.

And that's the kind of win that matters.

The Keynote Q&A Challenge: When Someone Publicly Dismissed the DARE Model

There's something uniquely vulnerable about standing on a stage, delivering your life's work to a room full of people, and having someone challenge you in real time.

Not in a hallway, not on an anonymous comment card, but live, on mic, in front of 1500 people.

It was during the Q&A portion of one of my keynotes. I had just walked the audience through the DARE model—Describe, Acknowledge, Review, Engage. I was feeling good. The energy in the room was high, heads were nodding, and people were leaning in. Then it happened.

During Q&A, a man stood up, took the mic, and with all the confidence of someone who had just won gold at the Olympics, he asked:

Do you think we really have time to do all of this?

Now, let's pause right there. If I had been listening to respond, my mind would've immediately gone to defensiveness. My internal narrative would have interpreted his neutral question as an attack. My prefrontal cortex would have shut down, and I would have launched into a rebuttal, pulled out stats, maybe tightened my tone, and said something about how *"making time for effective communication saves you ten times more on the back end."*

I would've "won" the point but lost the room. After spending 45 minutes talking about the importance of listening, not interpreting…I would have done everything I said not to do.

Instead, I engaged.

Not just politely. Not performatively. But fully.

I asked him a question—not to trap him, not to embarrass him, but to get us both into the same conversation.

"Is your concern that the model doesn't work, or that you don't have the time?"

He paused, visibly taken off guard. "I don't know if it works," he said. "I just know it takes too long."

Now we were in it: not a debate or a standoff. We were in the best thing to be in when you disagree: we were in a *dialogue*.

I followed up: "How many times have you used the DARE model?"

He smirked. "None."

I offered, "So can we agree that you're not yet in a position to speak to the efficacy or the time requirements of the model?"

He chuckled along with the audience, and just like that, the tension in the room shifted.

But I didn't stop there. Because *winning* wasn't the goal, *connection* was.

So I said this: "Your concern is valid. Time is a real factor. And it's a fair question—how do we practice this model when the clock is ticking and the pressure is high? Let me show you."

And in front of the room, I walked him, and everyone else, through a real-world, time-sensitive use of the DARE model– the very conversation we were having! I turned back to the audience and narrated, moment by moment, what just happened in our exchange:

- When I asked the first question? That was **Describe**.

- When I acknowledged his time concern as valid? That was **Acknowledge**.

- When I asked how many times he'd used the model? That was **Review**.

- And when I invited him and the audience to walk through it together? That was **Engage**.

I used the model without ever saying the words.

And the room saw it.

They didn't just hear about conversational competence; they *witnessed* it. They watched the DARE model in action. Watched a potentially tense exchange turn into a teachable moment, watched a dismissive audience member transform into a curious participant.

And you know what they remembered? Not that I had the perfect answer.

They remembered that I didn't rush, that I didn't try to win, rather, that I stayed in the conversation and invited someone else to do the same.

Here's why I'm sharing this with you. Because what happened in that room isn't magic. It's not charisma. It's not quick wit or stage presence or luck.

It's *practice*. It's the result of years spent learning the difference between defending myself and deepening the dialogue. Years spent rewiring my own habits, from being the "answers woman" to becoming someone who could sit in the discomfort of disagreement without needing to dominate.

This is what it means to engage: to participate in a conversation where the outcome isn't certainty, it's clarity. Where you don't have to agree, but you do have to *show up*. Where the other person doesn't need to be converted, but they do need to be *considered*.

That's what this whole chapter has been about, and what most hard conversations are missing.

If you're not willing to slow down, if you're not open to really listening, if you're not able to let go of the need to win or defend or be right, you're not engaging. You're just performing. I don't want you to perform, I want you to connect, and I want you to *practice*.

Because the truth is, the DARE model doesn't require perfect conditions. It doesn't require extra time. It requires intention.

That's it.

Think back on everything we've talked about in this chapter:

- That wedding where everyone wanted to be heard and no one remembered why they were there in the first place?

- The moments where "winning" cost more than it was worth?

- The difference between hearing and *understanding*?

- The power of the 5-second rule?

- The hard lesson of learning when to shut up.

- They all lead here.

To the moment where you stop using conversation as a weapon or a podium, and start using it as a bridge to the moment where you stop trying to convert people, and start trying to *connect* with them.

To the moment you **engage**.

Chapter 6 Recap: Engage for Conversation, Not Conversion

Cliff Notes, Dethra-Style:

If a wedding toast, a project meeting, and a keynote mic-drop taught us anything, it's this: most conversations fall apart because people stop trying to connect and start trying to conquer. We've confused engagement with performance, and listening with waiting for our turn. But here's the shift: when you engage for *conversation*, not *conversion*, you create space for truth, trust, and transformation. You don't have to agree. You don't have to surrender. But you do have to show up, shut up (yes, really), and *stay in it*. That's the real power move.

Key Takeaways:

- **Winning a conversation isn't the goal**—understanding and clarity are.

- **Position vs. Interest**: Don't get stuck on what someone says they want. Ask why they want it and see where your whys align.

- **People cling to being right** even after being proven wrong because the ego doesn't like losing. Engagement disrupts that reflex.

- **Listening to understand requires openness.** You don't have to agree, but you have to be curious.

- **Listening to respond is performance.** Listening to understand is presence.

- **Engagement means using your voice *after* you've used your brain and heart.**

- That one keynote challenger? He wasn't converted, but he was heard. And that's why the room shifted.

Why This Matters:

We are in a world that's louder than ever and still not hearing each other. In our relationships, our workplaces, and even our internal dialogues, we default to defensiveness, speed, and control. But leadership, connection, and change don't happen at that speed. They happen at the speed of trust. And trust is built when people feel seen, heard, and respected. The Engage step is where the DARE model becomes *real*. It's where it moves from mindset to mouth. From thought to action. From silence to *skillful speech*. If you skip this step, you're not avoiding conflict—you're inviting it to grow in the dark.

Call to Action:

In your next tough conversation, pause and ask yourself:

- "Am I listening to understand, or just waiting to respond?"

- "What's the real interest here, not just the position?"

- "Am I showing up to connect, or to win?"

Then engage, not to convert to but to connect and contribute because that's how real conversations *and real change* begin.

Part III

Executive Summary: Applying the D.A.R.E. Model in Real Life

Knowing the D.A.R.E. Model is one thing. Living it is another.

That's what this section is about: application. Because insight without action is just information and you didn't come this far for theory. You're here to change the way you lead, love, parent, speak, and show up when it counts.

Part III is where the rubber meets the road. Where high-stakes moments become opportunities and where I show you how to stop defaulting to avoidance, overreaction, or passive-aggression, and start practicing intentional, skillful dialogue. This is the part that makes the D.A.R.E. Model more than a framework; it makes it your practice.

What You'll Learn

Chapter 7: "Using the Model at Work," we walk straight into the boardroom and the breakroom. You'll learn how to manage up, down, and across with conversational competence. We cover how to:

- Give (and receive) feedback without flinching

- Get clarity from that *very* vague boss

- Handle performance reviews, leadership tensions, and team dynamics like a pro

You'll see what it looks like when a whole company transforms its culture through D.A.R.E., and You'll get plug-and-play templates for better conversations at every level of your organization, whether you're in positional authority or not. Because let's face it, the ROI on good communication is real and can be calculated.

Chapter 8: "Using the Model in Relationships," we get personal. Because the model isn't just for the office, it's for the living room as well. It's for the kitchen table, the group chat, the moment you and your spouse lock eyes and both know, this one might go left.

We show you how the D.A.R.E. Model can save your marriage, enhance your parenting, and add depth to strained connections. You'll explore the role of vulnerability, what it means to acknowledge without losing yourself, and how to talk to kids and teens when the topic is…well, hard. There's even a list of conversation starters to help you go deeper without going nuclear.

Chapter 9: "Using the Model in High-Stakes Conversations." Welcome to the hot zone!

This is where D.A.R.E. becomes your superpower in the moments that matter most: political debates, racial and social justice conversations, cultural identity, and community tension. You'll learn how to:

- Stay grounded when things get heated

- Talk about race without going silent or shouting

- Model grace, courage, and competence when others are watching

You'll also get a practical tool to prepare for high-stakes moments before they happen—so you can lead, not just react.

Chapter 10: "Making D.A.R.E. a Way of Life," we close strong by helping you embed this model into your everyday rhythm. You'll shift from reacting to responding. From avoiding to engaging. From surviving conversations to transforming them.

We'll guide you through your personalized D.A.R.E. Conversation Challenge because theory won't change your life, but practice will.

Why This Matters

It's not enough to know what to say. You have to build the muscle to say it when it counts.

This part of the book helps you *operationalize* the model. At work, at home, and everywhere in between. Because the places where you spend the most time are where your communication habits are built and either broken or transformed.

Every conversation is a chance to build trust, deepen understanding, and shift outcomes. But only if you've done the work.

That work starts here.

Why Now?

You don't have time to keep circling the same issues, avoiding the same people, or hoping that tension magically disappears. You're ready to take what you've learned and use it to create something different, on purpose.

This isn't about being perfect. It's about being better and better, which means saying what needs to be said, without burning everything down.

So here's your challenge: don't just read this part. Use it. Stretch yourself. Practice in the places that scare you. Be the person who brings clarity into chaos, connection into conflict, and courage into the conversation.

Let's D.A.R.E. to create better workplaces, relationships, and communities one conversation at a time.

Chapter 7

Conversational Competence Is a Leadership Skill

The Secret to Clearer Teams, Better Decisions, and Less Drama at Work

The Calendar Invite That Almost Cost a Career Win

Tasha didn't hate her job; in fact, she kind of loved it. Her position paid well, she had great benefits, her manager mostly stayed out of her way, and she was starting to get noticed in senior leadership meetings.

She was ambitious, intentional, and quietly building a name for herself, both at work and outside of it, where her coaching side hustle had developed a waitlist.

So when her manager, Carl, scheduled a last-minute "touch base" with no context and sent the invitation with the dreaded high-priority flag, Tasha immediately felt uneasy.

"Why is this urgent?"

"Why didn't he include a note?"

"Is this about that client call where I took over? Because I was saving the deal, not grandstanding."

The spiral came fast. The assumptions came faster.

By the time the five-minute reminder for the meeting popped up on her calendar, Tasha had:

Revised her résumé.

Checked the balance in her business bank account.

And halfway drafted her resignation letter, just in case Carl dropped a bomb.

But she still showed up. She joined the call early, camera on, posture tight, ready for whatever.

Carl opened with, "Hey, I just wanted to check in and say you handled that client call like a pro. Really appreciate how you stepped in. Have you ever thought about leading a few of those training sessions?"

Tasha blinked. Her heart did that little drop thing.

…Wait. What?

She unmuted. "Oh. Um… thank you?"

Carl nodded, oblivious. "That's all I had. Appreciate you."

Click. The meeting was over.

Tasha sat there for a full 30 seconds, stunned, not because she was wrong, but because she'd almost walked away from a job that was about to hand her a win. All because of a calendar invite… and an internal narrative she had accepted as fact.

Here's the thing: Tasha wasn't crazy. She was conditioned.

Her company had a pattern of last-minute "urgent" meetings that ended with:

"Thank you for your service, but you're no longer needed."

And her last manager was a master avoider who never had the courage to give feedback directly, so he'd schedule five-minute "check-ins" at the end of the day to drop bad news and dash.

Tasha had data to support her decision to brace for impact. But like most of us, she'd never been taught how to pause before she spiraled.

Tasha fell into a trap that swallows so many high-achievers: When no one's talking, we start writing the script ourselves, and usually cast ourselves as either the villain or the victim.

But here's what Tasha did next that changed everything. She texted her mentor, the one who had walked her through the Power Pivot strategy six months earlier, when she was at a critical crossroads in her career.

Her message said: "I spiraled today. It was bad. Almost sabotaged myself. Need to talk."

They met after work over tacos and a truth bomb or two. Her mentor said something that made Tasha perk up:

"You're not stuck. You're underdeveloped in two areas: conversational competence and managing up. I gave you the Power Pivot; now you need D.A.R.E. You're building empires outside the office but avoiding feedback inside it. That's a career-limiting move."

That night, Tasha found a notebook and wrote down the words:

D.A.R.E. to pause.

D.A.R.E. to check the story.

D.A.R.E. to lead your leader.

D.A.R.E. to speak up before spiraling.

And just like that, Tasha leveled up, not with a promotion or a raise, but with something way more powerful: the skill to own any room, rewrite the story, and stop sabotaging her seat at the table simply because she lacked conversational competence to manage up.

Tasha's breakthrough didn't just help her regulate her internal spiral; it marked the beginning of her learning how to manage up. She realized that waiting for her manager to communicate perfectly wasn't a strategy. If she wanted to lead from where she sat, she'd have to get intentional about how she received information, clarified expectations, and shaped the relationship going forward.

This is what conversational competence makes possible. And without it, even high-performing cultures lose their edge. Feedback becomes fear. Innovation turns into silence. And the best people leave not because of bad work, but because of bad communication.

Managing Up – Leading from Where You Sit

Managing up is not a cute career tip. It's a survival skill. If you're trying to grow in your role, get noticed for opportunities, or move on to your next level, you have to stop treating your manager like a mystery to be solved and start treating them like a relationship to be managed.

Most people make two huge mistakes when it comes to managing up:

1. **They don't do it.** They think management only flows downward.

2. **They announce it like it's a fight, leaving the airport.** Instead of treating it like a flight announcement, managing up should be treated like a good pair of Spanx; we are all wearing them, but no one feels the need to announce it.

Instead of walking around saying, "I'm managing up now!" just do it –strategically, intentionally, quietly, and with the outcomes to show for it.

Because here's the truth: The people who get promoted, who get access, who get tapped for special projects, they're not just good at their jobs. They're good at making sure their managers know exactly what value they bring and feel comfortable saying it in rooms where decisions are made.

What It Really Means to Manage Up

Managing up means actively creating the culture of your relationship with your manager.

It means:

• Setting the tone for how you want to communicate

• Helping your leader set realistic expectations for you

• Making it easy for them to see, articulate, and advocate for your value

If that sounds like a lot, it should. You're not there to be a cog in a wheel; you are there to be a **career CEO.**

One of the core philosophies I teach in my previous book, *Unstuck: Discovering Career Limiting Actions,* and our Employeepreneur™ program is this:

"You are a multi-billion dollar organization, and your career is your product. If your boss is the only one driving your product to market, you're already losing."

Managing up doesn't mean sucking up. It means:

- Thinking like a peer, even if you're not on the org chart
- Understanding your manager's goals, stressors, blind spots, and strengths
- Operating in a way that helps them win *and* positions you as valuable

It's a strategic exchange: You make their life easier. They make your career visible.

The Myth of Meritocracy

Let's bust a dangerous myth right now: "If I do good work, they'll notice."

No, they won't. I mean, occasionally they will, but not always, not consistently. And definitely not in a way that leads to opportunity. What they will notice is that work is getting done, as it should.

Your manager has 1,000 things on their plate. They're juggling their own projects, their own boss, their own insecurities, and a team full of people expecting them to lead with clarity and care.

You doing your job well makes them comfortable. But comfort doesn't always equal advocacy.

And here's the part no one says out loud: Your manager might *love* having you on the team because you make their job easier. That doesn't mean they're thinking about your next promotion.

They might even actively want to keep you where you are because you're so good.

So, if you think your excellence will automatically translate into advancement, that's not a career strategy. That's a narrative you've accepted as fact.

D.A.R.E. in Action: The Feedback Was Quiet—But the Damage Was Loud

One of my clients, let's call her Sheldon, had a manager who would never confront her directly. Instead, he'd make little comments, laughing as he said them, like:

"Somebody was feeling really confident in that meeting today, huh?"

Or…

"Interesting choice of words in that email you sent out…"

He never gave direct feedback, never followed up, never clarified what, if anything, needed to change. Instead, Sheldon would hear secondhand that her manager had concerns. Or worse, she'd get passed over for stretch assignments without knowing why.

By the time she came to me, she was ready to quit, but we used the D.A.R.E. Model to help her have the conversation instead.

Here's how she did it:

- **Describe:** She didn't accuse him of avoiding her. She said:

  "In my six months working with you, I've only gotten feedback from you twice, but I've received messages from colleagues at least seven times saying you had a concern about my work."

- **Acknowledge:** She named the discomfort head-on.

  "I don't like confrontation either, and you're probably right, I don't want to hear I've done a bad job. But what I dislike even more is being stuck in my career."

- **Review:** Sheldon challenged two narratives:

  1. "Managers don't care. They just want the work done."

  2. "If I speak up, I'll be labeled difficult."

Both stories had been running the show in her head. But once she questioned them, she realized they weren't based in truth but in fear.

- **Engage:** She had the conversation. Nervous, yes. But she separated herself from the outcome.

Her goal wasn't to win; it was to connect, clarify, and strategize for a better future working relationship and a clearer path to advancement.

And guess what? Her manager apologized. He explained that he thought indirect feedback was "easier" and didn't realize it was doing more harm than good. They agreed on a monthly check-in. Within two months, Sheldon was asked to co-lead a client pitch.

Why Review and Engage Are the Hardest When Managing Up

Of all the steps in the D.A.R.E. Model, Review and Engage are the hardest when it comes to managing up.

Why? Because reviewing your internal narrative means examining deeply embedded stories about power, permission, and value.

Some of those stories go so far back they don't even have words, just feelings. You feel uneasy around certain types of leaders, but don't realize it stems from something your grandmother said when you were five.

You act small around certain managers because you were once punished for "being too much." You defer to people who remind you of a teacher who never liked you. You've been telling yourself, *"This is just who I am."* But sometimes, "who you are" is just a 40-year-old story you never challenged. Managing up forces you to face that.

And Engage? Whew. That's the leap. That's when all your thoughts, all your fears, all your drafts have to become words. And words have consequences.

So yes—it's hard. But it's also where the growth lives.

Managing up is executive behavior. It isn't extra credit. It's not a "nice-to-have" leadership skill. It's how people at every level stay visible, valuable, and in control of their narrative and career advancement.

The D.A.R.E. Model doesn't just help you survive tough conversations. It enables you to build better relationships with the people who decide your next move. Whether you're brand new to your role or gunning for the C-suite, one truth remains:

If your manager can't clearly speak to your value, they can't advocate for you. And if you can't speak to it yourself, you're leaving your career to chance.

So before you complain about your boss again, ask yourself:

- Have I described what I need?
- Have I acknowledged where they're coming from?
- Have I reviewed the story I'm telling about them and me?
- Have I engaged them directly?

If not... you're not stuck.

Managing Down – Building the Culture You Want to Work In

If "managing up" is about helping your manager help you, then managing down and across is about creating a culture where everyone gets better because of how you show up.

That's right, you don't need a fancy title to be a culture shifter. You just need conversational competence and the courage to use it.

This section is for the people who lead others, mentor peers, or find themselves constantly saying, *"Why doesn't anybody just say what needs to be said?"*

Welcome to your section.

Managing Down – Leading People, Not Just Projects

Let's start with the hard truth: Some of the most significant workplace communication breakdowns happen between leaders and the people they manage, not because the leader is bad. Sometimes, it's because they were promoted for their skills, not their people sense. As a matter of fact, people knew they lacked people skills, but did nothing to address this deficiency. Other times, it's because they were never trained to lead humans: they lack patience, people skills or empathy. It is clear that they can manage tasks, KPIs, and projects, but people management is a challenge.

If you're leading a team, even a small one, you are now in charge of conversations that build trust, clarity, and accountability. And trust me, you can't automate that.

Here's what managing down really means:

- Giving feedback that's useful, not vague

164

- Creating psychological safety so people can speak freely for the purpose of advancing the team and the team's outcomes

- Describing what you want instead of reacting to what you didn't get

- Taking ownership when your team misses the mark because your instructions weren't clear

A lot of leaders skip this because it's hard. It requires emotional labor, patience, and humility. But *this* is where the real power of D.A.R.E. shows up in leadership.

D.A.R.E.-ing Down the Ladder

Let's walk through what D.A.R.E. looks like when managing down:

- **Describe** – Say what happened without assigning blame. *"The report was submitted two days after the deadline and without the updated figures from finance."*

- **Acknowledge** – Recognize the humanity in the situation. *"I know you've been juggling multiple deadlines, and the finance team was delayed getting you the numbers."*

- **Review** – Challenge the narrative. *"I caught myself making assumptions about your work quality, but realized that I hadn't given you a clear backup plan for when those numbers weren't in."*

- **Engage** – Open the floor. *"Let's talk about what needs to change so this doesn't keep happening. What support do you need from me next time?"*

This isn't about coddling. It's about clarity and growth.

To build a high-performing team, you must be a high-performing communicator.

Leadership Gut-Check:

- Are your team members clear on your expectations?

- Do they understand how their work contributes to larger organizational goals?

- Have you ever asked them what they need from you to do their job better?

If not, it's time to sharpen your conversational competence to become a more effective leader and guide direct reports to become fully engaged and clear about your shared goals.

What Happens When You Don't Manage Down

Let me tell you what happens when you don't manage down well.

People:

- Make up stories about what you think of them
- Feel anxious, unseen, or micromanaged
- Start doing just enough to avoid correction
- Quit… and not just the job—sometimes they quit trying

Managing down isn't just about delegation; it's where communication becomes culture.

And most of the time? It's not one big mistake that sinks the ship. It's the buildup of small, unclear, unspoken moments.

Managing Across – Navigating Power, Politics, and Peers

Now let's talk about managing across: the thing no one trains you for, but everyone expects you to be good at.

You've got peers who don't technically have authority over you, but still have power. You've got cross-functional teams with conflicting goals and clashing personalities. You've got people who talk over you, ignore your emails, and take credit for your ideas.

And through it all, you're supposed to "collaborate effectively."

Let's be honest—this is where it gets real.

Managing across means learning how to:

- Influence without authority

- Disagree without creating drama

- Speak up without sounding defensive

- Protect your value without burning bridges

D.A.R.E. is *crucial* here because the stakes are slippery.

When you're dealing with a peer who keeps stepping on your toes, there's no official power structure to fall back on. You can't "pull rank." You can't "write them up." And you definitely don't want to be seen as the colleague who runs to the boss every time things get tough-or worse, as the employee who can't hold their own in the eyes of leadership.

What you can do is describe what's happening, acknowledge the shared goal, review what stories might be getting in the way, and engage with clarity and confidence.

When I coach teams in this method, I provide this quick prompt to help you determine what unreviewed narratives may be getting in the way:

What's your default story about your peers? Do you assume they're competitors? Distractions? Roadblocks?

What if they're actually the *audience* for your next opportunity?

After that, you can Engage with this quick plug-and-play template for your next across-the-aisle convo:

"I've noticed [*concrete example*]. I know we're both committed to [*shared goal*]. I've been telling myself [*honest narrative*]. But I'd like to make sure we're aligned going forward by [*proposed solution or next step*]."

This works in person, over email, or even in a Slack message—tone is everything.

The Passive-Aggressive Peer: Diffusing Peer Conflict with D.A.R.E.

Let's say you have a colleague, Shae, who consistently volunteers for joint projects, then dominates every meeting as if it were a solo act.

You're tired of it, but you also don't want to sound petty.

Here's what a D.A.R.E. conversation could look like:

- **Describe**: *"In the last three meetings, I noticed that you've led most of the talking points and made the final recommendations without us recapping our shared input first."*

- **Acknowledge**: *"I know you care about the quality of our work and that you're excited to share ideas—we both are."*

- **Review**: *"What I caught myself thinking was that you don't see value in my input. But I also realized I haven't said anything about how I'd like to contribute."*

- **Engage**: *"Going forward, can we align beforehand on who shares what and how we present our recommendations as a team, allowing a different member of the team to lead each time?"*

This isn't confrontation: it's communication with purpose.

Everyone suffers the cost of avoiding these conversations:

- Projects get slowed down by politics

- Brilliant ideas die in silence

- You get left out of key conversations because no one knows what you stand for

You don't need to be best friends with everyone at work.

But if you want to lead, influence, and grow, you have to know how to communicate with, activate, and engage peers without positional authority. The D.A.R.E. model is your playbook. Where you sit on the org chart, you are responsible for the culture you create through your conversations. So don't wait for someone to hand you permission to lead. Use D.A.R.E. to claim it—in every direction.

D.A.R.E. to Handle Performance Reviews, Difficult Feedback & Leadership Tension

Let's talk about the conversation everybody hates and nobody prepares for: yes, this is hyperbole. I know some of you live for performance evaluations, and you spend all year planning for them. This section is for the rest of us.

Let's set the stage:

You're called in for your performance review. The energy in the room is… polite. Your manager slides a form across the table, says something generic like, "You've had a solid year," then adds a few vague suggestions about "stepping into leadership more" or "being more strategic." You nod. They nod. Someone says something about Q4 goals. You sign the paper. You both leave the room—and neither of you is better for the experience.

Sound familiar?

Now let's be clear: performance reviews *should* be valuable. They should feel like a GPS recalculation, not a courtroom sentencing. But most of the time, they're awkward, undercooked, and two steps behind reality.

The problem isn't just the performance evaluation itself; it's the way we've been taught to deliver and receive feedback about performance.

Here's the setup: For 12 months, no one gives honest feedback. At best, you get a "good job" in passing in the hallway. Then, one day, after 12 months…*surprise!* You're called in to discuss your growth, your gaps, and your goals in one uncomfortable 30-minute sit-down.

No wonder people check out, tear up, or turn defensive. Even managers hate them. According to a Harvard Business Review study, over a third of U.S. firms have scrapped annual reviews altogether. And for good reason—employees who receive frequent, meaningful feedback are 80% more likely to be engaged at work. Not once-a-year reports. Not rushed scorecards. Feedback.

The D.A.R.E. Approach to a Better Review

Performance conversations don't have to be painful. They just need structure and humanity. That's where D.A.R.E. comes in.

Let me show you what that looks like in a real moment.

The Feedback Nobody Wants to Hear

Manager: "In the presentation last week, you came across as emotionally detached. It felt like you weren't there."

Most people freeze, defend, or fake a smile and never ask to present again. But here's a D.A.R.E.-powered response that can *change a career*:

D – Describe: "I heard you say I seemed emotionally disconnected during the presentation. That feedback landed hard, but I appreciate the honesty. Can you tell me what you saw that gave you that impression?"

A – Acknowledge: "I take pride in showing up with presence, especially in high-visibility rooms. So if that didn't translate, I want to change my approach by understanding what I did and making the necessary adjustments."

R – Review: "The audience was from engineering, and I've heard over and over that they want 'just the facts, no fluff.' That was what I attempted to deliver. I now see that narrative may not have served me well."

E – Engage: "Next time, I'd like to find a better balance. If you're open to it, I'd love some feedback after my next presentation, specifically on presence. I want to grow here."

That's not an excuse. That's insight. That's clarity. That's leadership.

Difficult Feedback Deserves Depth, Not Drama

People often ask: *What do I do when I have to give tough feedback?*

You do exactly what you'd want someone to do for you:

- Tell the truth.

- Do it early.

- Wrap it in clarity, not cruelty.

Tough feedback becomes toxic when it's hoarded, sugarcoated, or weaponized. It becomes transformational when it's specific, direct, and in service of growth. Feedback isn't a form; it's a culture and a practice.

So no more generic: "You need to be more strategic." Try D.A.R.E.: "In client meetings, I notice you focus on the task list but rarely connect it to the bigger, long-term goal. Let's work on linking your execution to vision so people see your leadership."

That's a gift, that's actionable. That's a pat on the back, not a vague directive that eventually leads to a gut punch.

And Then There's Leadership Tension

Let's not pretend performance tension only flows one way. Sometimes, the most challenging performance conversation you'll have is with your boss or another leader at your level. And when they fail to manage expectations clearly or provide feedback consistently? It gets messy.

I coached a client once who said, "My manager only gives feedback in sarcasm. I never know if I'm succeeding or on the chopping block."

We crafted a D.A.R.E. conversation.

D – Describe: "I've noticed most of the feedback I receive is through quick jokes or comments in front of others."

A – Acknowledge: "I know humor can lighten the mood, and you've got a lot on your plate. However, this type of feedback leaves me unsure about how I am doing and how I may improve."

R – Review "I caught myself thinking I'm being set up to fail or that I'm not seen as someone who takes things seriously. But I also realize I've never asked for direct feedback in a 1-on-1 setting."

E – Engage "Would you be open to having a brief monthly check-in where we talk candidly about what's working and what needs to shift?"

It worked. Not because the manager changed overnight but because the dynamic did.

If you take nothing else from this section, take this: Performance conversations are not about the paperwork. They're about the relationship.

And your ability to navigate those moments, whether you're giving the feedback or receiving it, is what builds your reputation.

You don't need a title to be seen as a leader. You need presence, you need clarity, and you need a voice that knows how to D.A.R.E. in the moments that matter.

Case Study: The Company That Transformed Its Culture Using D.A.R.E.

When the conversations changed, everything changed.

That was the takeaway from a mid-sized technology firm we'll call PulseTech—a company known for rapid product innovation but plagued by communication breakdowns that cost them talent, time, trust, and money.

On paper, they had it all: solid revenue, strong branding, and competitive benefits, butut underneath the surface, the culture was cracked.

Their exit interviews told the story of silent tension and spiraling turnover:

- **"I never had a clue what my leader thought of my performance."** *I wasted months second-guessing instead of improving. That confusion cost the team momentum—and nearly cost me my job.*

- **"My manager avoided real feedback until it was too late."** *By the time I found out what needed to change, the decision had already been made. I wasn't coached—I was cornered.*

- **"There was so much tension across departments, we just avoided each other. We couldn't hit deadlines because no one wanted to collaborate, and our managers faked cohesion instead of fixing the fractures."** *Projects stalled, budgets blew up, and the customer experience suffered, all because grown adults were too afraid to speak directly.*

- **"I've never wanted people to argue so badly. Everyone smiles in meetings, but no one trusts each other. It's all politics and performance. It's exhausting."** *We were spending more energy managing perception than solving problems. And the business paid the price: we were losing good people left and right, and when they left, many great opportunities left with them.*

Worse, employee engagement scores had plummeted for three consecutive years. Turnover was highest among mid-level managers, those expected to bridge strategy and execution.

Their People & Culture leader called it "death by politeness." No one was yelling, because you would have to talk to yell, and they were not talking to one another..

So they called us in.

The Turning Point: Moving From Conflict Avoidance to Conversational Competence

Our first question wasn't: "What's wrong with your people?" It was: "What is the cost of this communication breakdown?"

That's the question that finally stopped the silence. Not the fluffy "culture" statements. Not the engagement survey. Not even the exit interviews, because by then, it was too late.

No, the turning point came when the leadership team saw the actual bill: missed deadlines, duplication of work, talent walking out the door, innovation stalling, and deals fumbled because departments weren't aligned.

No one cared when it was a people problem, so we showed them that it was a profit problem.

When we introduced the D.A.R.E. Model we didn't start with "communication training." We started with the cost of conflict avoidance. We showed them what happens when nobody says what they mean, when feedback is sugar-coated (or never delivered at all), and when meetings become performances instead of platforms for real solutions.

After several interviews and pulse-check surveys, we uncovered the dominant narratives holding the teams back at PulseTech:

- "Disagreement equals disrespect."

- "Feedback is dangerous."

- "If I speak up, I might lose my job."

- "If I push back, I'll be labeled difficult."

And the most damaging of all!: **"Silence is safety."**

These weren't policies; these were patterns, cultural stories passed down, absorbed, and reinforced through years of awkward reviews, unspoken team feuds, and a total absence of safe language or results from disagreement.

The Intervention: Embedding the D.A.R.E. Model in the Culture

We didn't just conduct a one-day workshop and then disappear. We partnered with leadership to embed the D.A.R.E. model into the company's communication, feedback, and decision-making practices over a 12-month transformation cycle.

Here's how:

1. Leadership First, Always

We began with a 2-day executive retreat. Not to "train," but to *untrain*. We had to unpack how their own communication styles shaped what the rest of the organization mimicked.

One VP said, "I realize now, I only give feedback to the people I like. The others? I just hope they figure it out or go away."

That admission changed everything.

We walked the exec team through live D.A.R.E. conversations with role-plays and real-time coaching:

- **Describe** without blame.
- **Acknowledge** tension *and* shared goals.
- **Review** personal narratives and unspoken rules.
- **Engage** in conversation, not compliance.

They left with a new mandate: lead with clarity and courage or reassess if leadership is for you.

2. Middle Managers as Culture Carriers

Next, we trained 140 people managers in how to use D.A.R.E. in three critical spaces:

- Performance conversations
- Cross-functional collaboration
- Managing up and across

We gave them tools, but more importantly, we gave them language.

Soon, "Let's D.A.R.E. this conversation" became a shorthand across departments.

One team even created a "D.A.R.E. Zone", a Friday drop-in hour for tough convos, cross-team feedback, and realignment.

3. Codifying D.A.R.E. into Systems

Culture change dies in ambiguity. So PulseTech made D.A.R.E. real:

- Every performance review began with a D.A.R.E. reflection.

- Conflict mediation included D.A.R.E. coaching.

- New leader onboarding included D.A.R.E. training within 30 days.

Even Slack channels adopted it:

#D.A.R.E.-to-ask

#D.A.R.E.-to-feedback

#D.A.R.E.-to-align

It wasn't about a model; it was about a culture shift in the organization.

The Impact: From Fearful to Fearless Conversations

Twelve months after the implementation of D.A.R.E., PulseTech had numbers that told a powerful story:

- Employee engagement rose by **22%**

- Retention of high-performing managers increased by **37%**

- Interdepartmental project delays dropped by **41%**

Now, I'm not one of those consultants who paint transformation as neat and painless. So while I'm proud to report those results, let me also tell you about the mess it took to get there because change is rarely smooth, and fundamental culture shifts come with growing pains.

Some people came kicking and screaming. Others opted not to come at all.

One C-suite executive stood up in a leadership session and flat-out said, "This is a waste of time and money. You're just here to cash a check and leave." Ironically, that same leader became one of the biggest advocates for the D.A.R.E. Model nine months later.

Another senior leader made their stance crystal clear: they liked the old way. They weren't interested in being part of an organization that, in their words, "encouraged discord." They resigned and took a small faction of loyal followers with them.

Turnover got worse before it got better. Within the first few months of implementation, voluntary and involuntary exits spiked. Leaders panicked. Some whispered, "Did we break the culture?" But the truth was this: D.A.R.E. didn't break the culture. It revealed it.

The D.A.R.E. model unearthed performance issues that had been quietly draining the organization for years. It exposed where conflict avoidance had enabled poor work, protected underperformance, and sustained something the HR team jokingly started calling "employment sustained by hope."

Let me explain.

Employment Sustained by Hope

This was the phrase that circulated during the second quarter of D.A.R.E. implementation. We discovered a sizable group of employees who were still on payroll, not because they were contributing, but because their managers *hoped* they would get better.

No coaching. No clear KPIs. No direct feedback. In some cases, *no job description*.

Managers admitted they kept these employees around because it was easier than confronting the issue. One even said, "He was a great candidate with a bright future. I knew he could do the job; he just needed it to click. I kept waiting for him to wake up one day and just be better."

When we brought those employees into honest D.A.R.E. conversations, the results were telling.

- Some said, "I didn't even want this role—I just needed a job."

- Others acknowledged they didn't have the skills or drive to meet expectations.

- A few felt betrayed and opted to leave, not because of the feedback itself, but because it had been withheld for so long. They no longer trusted leadership.

176

Performance conversations finally started happening, and they actually *meant* something. Some employees turned a corner with clear coaching and structure in place. Others were guided through performance improvement plans. And yes, some were let go; not out of punishment, but out of a failure to meet performance goals.

Everyone Wanted to Be Held, But Not Held Accountable

D.A.R.E. sounded great in theory.

People LOVED quoting it.

"Review the narrative!"

"Engage, not convert!"

But when it was *their* narrative under review? That's when the tension showed up.

You could see the fake smiles, those tight-lipped "I want you to drop dead" grins when someone was challenged to actually *practice* what they'd been preaching. One employee shouted during training, "I know this is going to be amazing eventually, but I hate this sh!+ right now!"

And honestly? I loved that moment. Because that's when I knew we were getting somewhere.

Change Isn't Clean, It's Messy, Necessary, and Worth It

There's no fairy dust in the D.A.R.E. model. Just real conversations, real reflection, and a lot of courageous discomfort.

But the real win? The qualitative shift. Leaders began saying things like:

- *"My team finally tells me the truth."*
- *"I am looking forward to feedback from my supervisor."*
- *"We disagree faster, better, and the results are amazing."*

Employees began reporting that they felt:

- Safer

- Heard

- Respected

Some of you are thinking that all sounds good, but I need more than safe, heard, and respected because none of those are budget items on the P&Ls. Let's talk about how this implementation showed up on the P&Ls: The 3 P's.

What Happened to the 3 Ps: Performance, Productivity, and Profits?

- **Performance** improved by 28%, as measured by goal attainment and year-over-year quality metrics.

- **Productivity** rose by 19%, measured through output per team and time-to-completion benchmarks.

- And yes, **profits** increased by 16.35% in just 12 months.

And no, we didn't have to do a complete reorg or hire a new fleet of high-priced consultants. The shift came because people finally had a common language for conflict and clarity. The D.A.R.E. model gave them the framework and the permission to stop pretending and start producing.

D.A.R.E. didn't just improve communication. It redefined what *good culture* looked like, and good culture is always about improving the work environment to enhance the work product.

It reminded leaders and employees alike that high performance doesn't have to come at the cost of humanity and that conversational competence isn't optional; it is essential.

In the end, it wasn't just a shift in dialogue; it was a shift in identity. Once a company creates a culture where people know how to communicate effectively, that company is unstoppable.

Culture Change Is a Conversation Strategy

What PulseTech proved is what we've known all along:

You don't change culture with posters and pizza parties: you change it with conversations.

D.A.R.E. gave them a framework for those conversations. Not to avoid conflict, but to use it. Not to keep the peace, but to build it. Because every policy, every meeting, every team is only as strong as the conversations that hold it together.

Chapter 7 Recap: Managing in All Directions—Without Losing Your Mind (or Your Cool)

Cliff Notes, Dethra-Styles:

Managing up, down, and across isn't just corporate speak; it's survival. If you've ever left a meeting thinking "did we all just agree to nothing?" or replayed a conversation with your boss like it was a breakup text, this chapter was for you.

Here's the truth most folks don't tell you: leadership isn't just positional, it's conversational. And managing your manager (which is advisable), leading your team (without power trips), and working with your peers (without plotting revenge in the group chat) all come down to how you show up in conversation.

D.A.R.E. gave you the blueprint.

We busted the myth that good work speaks for itself. We exposed the damage of saying nothing, hoping it gets better. (It won't. Hope is not a management strategy.) And we showed you how to speak up, strategically, respectfully, powerfully, at every level with simple conversational competence.

Key Takeaways:

- **Managing up** isn't sucking up. It's setting your leader up to speak your name in rooms you can't enter, yet.

- **Managing down** isn't micromanaging. It's choosing clarity, care, and accountability over chaos and complaints.

- **Managing across** is about building bridges, not battlegrounds. Influence doesn't need a title.

- **Performance reviews** should not feel like getting ambushed in HR. Feedback is a gift, not a grenade.

- **The D.A.R.E. model isn't just for individuals.** It can (and has) shifted entire organizational cultures, because clear, confident communication is contagious.

- **Employment sustained by hope** is a real thing. And it's costing companies time, trust, and talent. We fix that with feedback, not fantasies.

Why This Matters:

You can't lead what you won't engage. You can't fix what you won't face. And you can't grow in silence.

Whether you're running a team or just trying to survive one, mastering the art of managing in all directions sets the tone for how people experience you—and how they *remember* you. Conflict-avoidant cultures don't produce high-performing teams. They produce resentment, rumors, and resignation letters.

The workplace is a web of conversations. When you learn to D.A.R.E. your way through the tough ones, you shift everything: morale, momentum, and money.

Call to Action:

Before your next conversation with your boss, your team, or that one peer who never quite "circles back," ask yourself:

- What's the narrative I've accepted as fact?

- Have I made it easy for this person to understand my value?

- Am I avoiding this conversation because it's hard or because I haven't prepared?

Then D.A.R.E. your way through it. Don't dominate or deflect. Just lead.

Because real leadership doesn't wait for a title; it starts with a conversation.

Chapter 8

From Tension to Truth: Using the D.A.R.E. Model to Strengthen Love, Family, and Friendship

The Group Chat Fallout

Let me tell you about the time I almost lost a 15-year friendship over a meme.

It started on a random Tuesday. I was minding my business and being productive when my friend, let's call her Danielle, dropped a meme in our shared friend group text. It was one of those passive-aggressive-but-funny ones that said:

"If you only call me when you need something, just say that."

Then she added the eyeball emoji. You know the one.

Now, here's the thing: I called Danielle that morning to ask if she could pick up something because I was stuck in back-to-back meetings, and I had to get the item that day or I would have to wait a week for another opportunity to get it. So naturally, I read the meme as if it were directed at me in the group chat.

I stared at it. Then stared at my phone. Then, reread our entire text history as if I were building a case for trial, and I was. It was a trial in my head where Danielle had no opportunity to present a case or mount a defense.

In my head, I said, "I know she didn't." So, I did what any emotionally mature adult should do.

I stopped responding and went silent….for two weeks.

No "hey, girl," no thumbs up on messages, no "did you see what happened the other day?" just radio silence. And the group noticed. People started texting me separately. "You good?" "Did something happen?" One friend even asked if I'd been kidnapped.

Finally, Danielle called me. I let it go to voicemail. Then she texted:

"Girl, what is going on? Are you upset about the meme from two weeks ago? Because I swear that meme wasn't about you."

And that's when I realized, I need D.A.R.E. as much as anyone else. D.A.R.E. is for all of us because, as you can see, I'd done all the things this book is trying to help all of us unlearn. I assumed. I interpreted. I made it deep. I wrote an entire screenplay in my head about betrayal, abandonment, and meme-based warfare without ever checking the facts.

Later, when we actually talked (yes, I used D.A.R.E. to get myself together), I described what I saw and how I felt. Danielle acknowledged that the timing made things look bad. She reminded me of all the times I showed up for her and did not hesitate to let me know how ridiculous I was being. No one cried. No one threw a phone. We laughed because that meme had been in her drafts for weeks, and she happened to pick that day to hit send.

Here's the thing: adult friendships can be fragile at times, not because people are bad friends, but because we carry unspoken expectations, unresolved stress, and a whole lot of "they should know better." D.A.R.E. gives us a different way.

Whether it's your spouse, your sister, or your brunch bestie, this chapter is for you.

Let's save some relationships.

D.A.R.E. to Be a Better Friend

Let's go ahead and say the quiet part out loud:

Some of us are bad friends, and I said "us" because we have all been a bad friend at one time or another.

But it's not because you don't care. It's because you never learned how to communicate when stuff gets weird.

Friendship, for most of us, was our first taste of chosen love. Not assigned love like family, but the kind we handpicked based on shared trauma in math class, a mutual love of Usher, or who had snacks on the school bus. Our friendships taught us what it meant to belong, to be liked, to be funny, to be trusted. But nobody ever pulled us aside and said,

"Hey. Here's how to talk to your friend when they hurt your feelings without turning it into a dramatic monologue with a soft R&B soundtrack playing in your head."

Enter: The D.A.R.E. Model.

You've seen how this model works at work, but this chapter is where we flip the script and use it in the places that matter most, where feelings are raw, stakes are high, and nobody's getting paid to be there.

Let's talk about the five ways people ruin good friendships, and how D.A.R.E. helps you save them before they flatline.

1. The Silent Treatment is Not a Conversation Strategy

Ghosting a friend after one weird comment at brunch is not communication, it's emotional avoidance dressed up in cute clothes.

D.A.R.E. Step: Describe.

Before you hit "Do Not Disturb" on your bestie, try describing what you noticed without accusations.

> "At lunch, when I was talking about my diagnosis, you spoke while I was speaking to talk about what was wrong with you. It made me feel like you were dismissing my diagnosis."

That's it. That's the whole sentence. No, "You always..." No, "See, this is why..."

Just a clear, neutral description of the moment that made you feel the way you felt.

Spoiler: Most friendship drama starts because someone interpreted a moment without clarifying it. D.A.R.E. invites you to step back from the interpretations and just start with what happened. This simple action allows each party to insert new data, clarify misconceptions, or apologize when they made a misstep.

2. Acknowledge Without Apologizing for Existing

Have you ever had a friend tell you their truth, and your gut response was to fix it, defend yourself, or change the subject?

We do it because discomfort makes us squirm. But D.A.R.E. says: acknowledge first, explain later.

D.A.R.E. Step: Acknowledge.

Acknowledgment sounds like:

"Hearing your diagnosis scared me. I did try to change the subject, and that was wrong. I should have handled my fear better."

Notice what it doesn't include:

- A rebuttal

- A resume of how good a friend you are

- A dramatic sigh followed by "I guess I'm just a horrible person"

Acknowledgment is not about self-sacrifice. It's about saying: "I see you. I hear you. And your experience is valid, even if it's different from mine."

3. Review the Story, Not Just the Scene

Let's say your friend forgot your birthday. Again. You are fuming. You are rehearsing your "I'm fine" voice that's laced with disappointment. You are about to become the villain in the next season of your friendship.

But wait.

D.A.R.E. Step: Review.

What's the narrative you're working with? Is it:

"She forgot because she doesn't care."

Or maybe, "She's been in survival mode lately, and it slipped through the cracks."

Review the stories you've accepted as fact. Check them. Ask:

- Have I been honest with myself about what I expect in friend-ship?

- Have I made those expectations clear, or just assumed they knew?

- Am I holding them to a standard I haven't explained?

D.A.R.E. invites you to review not only their behavior, but also your beliefs about it. Because sometimes, we're mad at people for breaking rules they don't know exist.

4. Engage Without Needing to Win

Here's the hard truth: You can "win" an argument and still lose a friendship. If your goal is to be right, prepare to be right alone.

D.A.R.E. Step: Engage.

Engaging means having the conversation not to convert or convince, but to connect. It sounds like:

"Can we talk about what's going on? I don't want this to turn into distance."

It also sounds like:

"I'm not mad. I'm hurt. And I want us to get back to laughing about nonsense again."

D.A.R.E. helps you engage with a purpose: not to dominate, but to restore. You're not coming to court. You're coming to the table. And preferably, there's wine or wings involved.

5. Don't Confuse Vulnerability with Weakness

One of the greatest lies adult friends tell is:

"I didn't want to say anything because I didn't want to start drama."

Let's be honest. That usually means:

"I didn't want to be vulnerable. I didn't want to be seen as needy. I didn't want to admit it bothered me."

But healthy friendships require vulnerability. Otherwise, you're both just smiling and simmering until it all explodes over something dumb, like a meme in a group chat.

Here's the plot twist: when you D.A.R.E. to be honest, to say the awkward thing kindly, to risk being misunderstood for the sake of being real, your friendships deepen.

Not everyone will meet you there. But the ones who do? They're your people. And together, you will all get through anything.

Friendship Check-In: A Mini Exercise

Here's a quick tool to use with your people. Try this over coffee, via text, or next time you're on vacation, spending money you don't need to spend.

Ask each other:

1. "What's something I do that makes you feel supported?"

2. "What's something I might not realize that hurts or annoys you?"

3. "How can we better show up for each other right now?"

Then D.A.R.E. your way through the answers:

- Describe what's working or not.

- Acknowledge the effort they've already made.

- Review assumptions you've had about each other.

- Engage in a plan to move forward, together.

Because here's the truth: Friendship is not sustained by history. It's sustained by honesty. And D.A.R.E. gives you the words to stay honest without burning everything down.

So before you block her, blast her, or blow up the chat, try one good, D.A.R.E. conversation.

You'd be amazed at what a little Describe, Acknowledge, Review, and Engage can do for your friendship.

Blood, Bruises, and Boundaries: Sibling Edition

Let me tell you about Isaiah and Mia.

They're siblings in that classic, can't-live-with-you-can't-live-without-you way. Born 18 months apart, they've been each other's first fight, first

188

snitch, and first partner in crime. Growing up, they were inseparable, matching Easter outfits, side-eyeing the auntie with the questionable cooking, and tag-teaming Saturday chores like a tiny cleaning crew with attitude, all so they could go outside and play.

But adulthood? That's where the plot thickened.

Both were brilliant students, with Mia always edging a little ahead academically. Isaiah went corporate while Mia went creative. Isaiah became spreadsheets and suits. Mia leaned into acrylics, affirmations, and freelancing. They didn't fall out, exactly… they just grew apart. Until one Thanksgiving, everything boiled over. And what caused the explosion?

A casserole.

Yes, a casserole. Specifically, Mia's sweet potato casserole that Isaiah declared tasted like "a warm apology for better food."

Everyone at the table laughed except Mia.

What they didn't know, what they *never* seemed to know, was that Mia had been up since 6 a.m., cooking every single dish from scratch. She wasn't just contributing dinner; she was trying to contribute *value*. She wanted to be seen as an adult, a contributor, as valuable and not just "the artsy one" or "Mia being Mia."

But Isaiah's little dig, masked as humor, hit a nerve that had been raw for years, not because of the casserole, but because of the *pattern*. Isaiah always had something to say about her life choices, her career path, her timeline. And Mia, being the peacemaker of the family, would just laugh it off, smile, swallow the sting, and keep it cute.

But this time? She didn't.

The next day, Mia sent a text, not a drag, not a dissertation. A D.A.R.E.

"At dinner, when you joked about my casserole, I felt dismissed. You laughed as if it were funny to you. Everything on your plate was made from scratch by my hands, and that moment mattered to me."

Isaiah didn't respond right away. Hours passed. Then, later that night, he called.

He didn't defend himself. He didn't get loud or dismissive. He apologized, not performatively, but sincerely. Then he got honest.

He admitted the jokes were his armor. Beneath the teasing lay his belief that Mia was brilliant and wasting her talent by selling art at festivals. He didn't understand her choices, and he probably never would. But the joke wasn't meant to hurt. It was just the only way he knew how to say what he actually felt.

And Mia? She received the honesty. It stung, sure, but she also saw the truth in it, not about her life choices, but about *his perspective.* She told him it hurt not to have his support, but she also told him this: to protect her peace and continue loving and respecting him, she'd need to create space, not out of punishment, but out of necessity.

She clarified: more space didn't mean less love, it just meant *better boundaries and more emotional protection for her.*

You wanted a happy ending? This is one.

It may not come with tears, Kumbaya, or a promise to call more often. But it came with truth, with clarity, and with D.A.R.E. in action. Sometimes, that's the conversation that needs to be had, and it's the most honest kind of love that families can offer each other.

D.A.R.E. is not about forcing a fairytale ending. It's about getting to the right ending, the one based on clarity, not mythology. It provides you with the tools to move forward with real information, not assumptions, and not just your hopes about how things should be. Sometimes that ending is reconciliation, and other times it's a respectful distance. But either way, it's built on truth, and that is the essence of the D.A.R.E. model.

Now, let's talk about how that truth plays out when you apply D.A.R.E. inside family dynamics: the expectations, the silence, the too-much-talking-but-not-enough-listening, and what it really means to engage with family when love exists alongside deep family wounds.

D.A.R.E. and Family: When Love Isn't the Same as Communication

Some of the most powerful words I ever heard in a song were in a song by India Arie. The opening line was:

One shot to your heart without breaking your skin. No one has the power to hurt you like your kin.

Those words nearly brought me to tears because they brought back all of the times I was hurt by family, comforted friends who felt betrayed by family, or I was the perpetrator of family hurt. The people closest to you can cause the deepest wounds.

But, before we get too deep, let's start here:

This is not a substitute for therapy. If you, your cousin, your daddy, or your grown daughter is willing to go to therapy, **GO!** Go with your whole heart, and take notes. Go even if you all still sit in the car in silence before going in. Go even if only one of you wants to be there. Therapy is not the enemy. Therapy is the team.

And.

Sometimes, you can't get the whole family to sit on a couch and hash it out with a licensed clinician. Sometimes, what you need isn't a full-on family intervention, just a way to have one good, guided, emotionally intelligent conversation without it ending in a three-week group text standoff or a full-blown family reunion boycott.

That's where D.A.R.E. comes in.

The D.A.R.E. Model won't fix your entire bloodline. But it *can* help you face the moments that blow up families more than anything else:

- Births that change the power dynamic
- Deaths that surface old resentments
- Money that disappears, or never appears
- Inheritances that get weird
- Siblings who don't speak but pretend for pictures
- Cousins who think "you changed" because you "got that degree"
- Spouses who just don't get along with your family members
- Group chats that feel like landmines

- That one uncle who no one will address, but every little girl in the family has been "cautioned" about him

Let's talk about it.

Why Families Struggle with Hard Conversations

You'd think that the people who raised you, know your allergies, and can recognize your baby picture with no label would be the best at tough conversations.

They're not.

According to a 2023 Pew Research Center survey, 42% of adults report being estranged or emotionally distant from at least one family member. That's nearly half of the population walking around with unresolved conversations in their bloodline.

Let that sit for a second.

Part of the reason is simple: family systems are emotionally loaded. We're not starting from neutral. We're starting from years, sometimes decades, of layered history, unspoken expectations, generational norms, inherited trauma, and "that's just how we are" energy.

We assume love should translate to understanding, but it doesn't. You can love someone deeply and still not know how to speak to them when things get hard. Especially when:

- Roles are rigid ("She's always been the sensitive one")

- Stories go unchallenged ("Well, you know how Daddy is…")

- Truth feels disloyal ("We don't talk about that outside the family.")

Family dynamics are where emotional shortcuts get coded into the culture. And once that shortcut is established —snark instead of honesty, silence instead of boundaries —it's hard to detour.

D.A.R.E. is your detour.

Yes. Now we're getting into the real meat of it.

D.A.R.E. in Action: When Grief, Money, and Family Collide

Let's be clear: no family gets through life drama-free.

The family group chat gets weird, the loaned money never gets paid back, the cousin who used to be your best friend still hasn't spoken to you, *even at the funeral*. And if you D.A.R.E. bring up boundaries at Thanksgiving, somebody's going to hit you with, "Here you go again with that therapy talk."

This section is not about the fairytale ending. It is about the formula to stop the cycle: the cycle of pretending everything's fine until it explodes into an *"I'm calling the police"* situation over something as simple as a pan of dressing.

Let's walk through five real family messes (not the edited-for-TV versions) and see what D.A.R.E. looks like in the middle of all that beautifully complicated chaos we call family drama.

1. The Will That Wrecked Thanksgiving

Big Mama died. And with her went the last thread holding some of the family dynamics together.

She left the house to the oldest child. A lump sum to the youngest—aka the golden child. And exactly **$0.00** to the cousin who lived with her, paid the bills, took her to every appointment, and changed every adult diaper for the last 18 months of her life.

To add insult to injury, the children who flew in *only* to claim their "inheritance" didn't even say thank you.

The real kicker? Big Mama told *everyone* her wishes: she made it clear at barbecues, at Bible study, at random moments in the living room that her one and only caretaker would receive something meaningful when she passed away. But nothing about that promise made it into ink. And now the family is in full turmoil.

Whispers, side-eyes, and group texts that have gone silent.

While the cousin is loudly expressing resentment and anger for the children not respecting Big Mama's wishes, the oldest sibling has taken to loudly reminding everyone that the only reason the cousin was living there in the first place was because they were *homeless*. According to the oldest child, now owner of the home, taking care of Big Mama was "the job"—and the payment was food and shelter; they are owed nothing.

The youngest, meanwhile, is unbothered and very clear: "I supported financially. I covered the gaps when social services fell short. That money? It's mine. I earned it."

And now, there's a family Zoom with lawyers that no one wants to attend but everyone knows they can't avoid.

Tension is high. Resentment is thick. And the grief that should have brought people closer is now tangled up in silence, side conversations, and subtle digs.

So how do you D.A.R.E. your way through a situation like this, especially if you are the cousin who feels slighted?

D.A.R.E. Moment: From the Cousin's Point of View

Describe: Describe vs Interpret

When the will was read and I wasn't included, I noticed that neither of you said anything about my role these last 18 months. I didn't hear a thank you, a conversation, or even a text after everything settled. That silence stood out to me.

(Notice: No assumptions. No, you don't care about me.' Just describing what happened and what didn't.)

Acknowledge similarities without minimizing differences:

I know this has been hard on all of us. We lost someone we each had a different relationship with. And I know everyone contributed in their way, financially, emotionally, and logistically. That's not lost on me. But my experience, being here every day, up close and personal with her decline, was different. I'm not asking you to agree with it, but I do need you to acknowledge that difference.

(It affirms their contributions without erasing the unique burden of caregiving.)

Review the narrative accepted as fact:

What's frustrating is hearing things like, 'You were just staying here because you needed a place to live.' That story makes it sound like I was freeloading instead of providing full-time care. However, that narrative overlooks the reality of what I did, managing her appointments, covering bills, and being her full-time caregiver when no one else was there. It erases the sacrifices, the labor, and the verbal promises we all heard but never wrote down.. It's a version that's convenient, but it's not true. And I don't think we can move forward if we're not willing to question the stories we've been telling ourselves.

(It gently challenges the false narratives that keep families stuck.)

Engage for conversation, not conversion:

I'm not here to change the will. And I'm not expecting everyone to agree with me. But I need to say this out loud: I gave a lot in those final years—my time, my money, my energy—and I believe that contribution should have been recognized. Just because it wasn't written down doesn't mean it didn't happen. I know I deserve acknowledgment for my work, and Big Mama deserves to have her wishes honored. Let's discuss this like the people she raised us to be. I'm not here to fight—I'm here because silence hasn't worked, and I don't want to keep carrying resentment in place of resolution.

(It opens the door to ongoing dialogue, not demands or ultimatums.)

Why This Matters:

No, this won't magically redistribute wealth. But it does begin the conversation that can prevent future family feuds, and in some families, *that* is revolutionary.

2. The New Baby and the Main Character Energy Shift

A new baby has arrived, and the family group chat is full of photos, hearts, and baby emojis. Everyone is cooing, posting, and scheduling visits.

Everyone... except the five-year-old.

The former center of the universe is suddenly quiet, clingy, and saying things like, "I wish the baby would go back in mommy's belly."

Mom is overwhelmed. Grandma is annoyed. Auntie is silently judging from across the room. But what no one is saying out loud is this: This child is grieving the loss of their position, their rhythm, and their role. And their feelings aren't being described; they're being dismissed.

Here's how a D.A.R.E.-based conversation might sound. This is the exact kind of conversation I had to have with my nephew when *he* lost his spot on the emotional throne.

D.A.R.E. Moment: Helping a Child Through a Role Shift

Describe vs. Interpret:

"When your baby sister came home, I noticed you stopped showing me your drawings. You also haven't wanted to play as much lately. Does something feel different for you?"

(Not: "You're being bad." Not: "You're jealous." Just: "Here's what I see." No judgment. No assumption.)

Acknowledge similarities without minimizing differences:

"It makes total sense to feel a little mad or sad. You love your baby sister, and you're also trying to get used to sharing attention. That's a lot for one person, especially when everything changed so fast."

(We acknowledge the shared love for the baby without glossing over the child's sense of loss.)

Review the narrative accepted as fact:

"I think grown-ups sometimes believe kids should just adjust quickly because 'they're young, they'll bounce back.' But that's not fair to you. You've had five years of being the only one. And it's okay to need time to get used to something so big."

(We challenge the tired adult narrative that emotional adjustment should be instant for children or that kids don't notice what's going on.)

Engage for conversation, not conversion:

"Can we make a new plan together? I want us to find one special thing that's just for you and me every week. You get to choose it. I just want to make sure you still feel seen, even with a new baby in the house."

(Not trying to fix the feeling. Just trying to stay connected while it gets processed.)

Why This Matters:

Because kids are people too, and people, even the smallest ones, deserve conversations that name the truth, hold space for the hard feelings, and remind them that change doesn't mean erasure.

When we use D.A.R.E. early, kids don't just learn how to manage conflict; they learn they *deserve* to be heard, even when life shifts. And they grow up less likely to bury their emotions in silence or act out because they never had language for what they felt.

3. The In-Law Standoff That Ended in Police and Potato Salad on the Floor

Your sister and your brother's wife don't get along. No one knows when it started, but everyone knows it is there. They've been "tolerating" each other for years, which in this family means surface smiles, side-eyes, and a cold war waged through passive-aggressive compliments and petty kitchen power plays.

But at the last family gathering, it wasn't subtle. It wasn't cute. It was *chaos.*

A snide comment turned into shouting. Shouting turned into shoving. A folding table was flipped. Potato salad hit the floor. Half the family packed up and left before dessert. Someone called the police– it got ugly.

Now, no one wants to host the next gathering because no one wants to answer the "Are they both going to be there?" question or choose who gets invited and who doesn't.

The family is fractured. The tension is unbearable. And you? You're stuck in the middle, trying to hold the pieces together while pretending you're not exhausted.

Here's how you might use the D.A.R.E. model, not to fix it, not to play mediator, but to start one honest conversation with your sister.

D.A.R.E. Moment: Talking to Your Sister After the Explosion

Describe vs. Interpret:

"At the last gathering, the conflict between you and her ended with the police being called. People left the house early. Our mom was embarrassed. The mood shifted, and the plans we had for a nice family gathering that went well into the night did not happen."

(Stick to what happened, not what you think it meant. No need to say "you caused a scene." Just describe the scene.)

Acknowledge similarities without minimizing differences:

"I know this relationship has been hard for a long time. I know you feel like she's never respected you, and I get why that's painful. And I also know *she* feels like you've never accepted her. This dynamic is heavy for everyone."

(Validate without excusing. You're not choosing sides, you're naming tension on both ends.)

Review the narrative accepted as fact:

"For years, we've all just chalked this up to 'that's just how they are,' like it's normal. But what happened last time made it clear: this isn't normal, and it's not sustainable. The belief that the rest of us should just absorb the tension to keep the peace? That's not working anymore."

(Challenge the story that silence equals peace and name the cost of not addressing it.)

Engage for conversation, not conversion:

"I'm not asking you to be best friends with her. I'm not even asking for reconciliation. I'm asking if you're willing to have one conversation, maybe with someone neutral present, to set ground rules for being in the same space. Not for her sake, but for the sake of the rest of us who love you, the family gatherings and you at the family gathering don't want to have to imagine a gathering where we have to choose who attends."

(Make it clear the goal isn't agreement—it's functional coexistence. You're not pushing for a resolution, just responsibility.)

Why This Matters:

D.A.R.E. doesn't require everyone to hug it out. It doesn't demand that you pretend decades of tension don't exist, but it does ask you to stop confusing emotional avoidance with peace, and to stop letting your love for one person silence your truth with another.

4. The Family Business Blowup

Your father built something, not just a business, but a *name,* a reputation, a legacy. He passed it down to his two daughters—you and your sister—after years of careful planning. No surprises, no drama, just vision, structure, and love. He spent *half his life* making sure the transition wouldn't feel like a handoff in the dark. His mantra was always the same:

"I want you girls to have options, and I want *happy* to be option number one."

He was clear: this was meant to be a gift, *not a weight.*

However, life changed, and the business remained the same.

Now, what would make you happiest —the thing that would let you take care of your health, your time, and your dreams—is selling the business and walking away with your peace *and* your share.

Your sister doesn't see it that way.

To her, selling the business is giving up on your father's name. She wants to grow it, modernize it, honor the legacy, and to do that, she needs *you.* Not just your signature, she needs your buy-in, your investment, your expertise, and your full attention. Now, every conversation ends the same. The polite ones are clipped and meaningless, and the real ones are heavy.

Your sister keeps saying:

"Daddy would be rolling in his grave."

And you keep saying:

"Daddy didn't want us to sacrifice everything to keep something going. He wanted us to be happy. And I'm not happy doing this anymore."

This isn't just about business; it's about *grief,* loyalty, exhaustion, and the version of success you were raised to chase, and now a legacy you may walk away from.

So what does it look like to D.A.R.E. through this?

D.A.R.E. Moment: From the Sister Who Wants to Sell

Describe vs. Interpret:

"Last time we talked about selling, the conversation ended with raised voices and no resolution. You said I was abandoning Dad's legacy, and I left feeling like my choice was either guilt or silence. That's not sustainable."

(Stick to what happened, not what you assume she believes. No, "you guilt-trip me." Just: "Here's what happened and how it landed.")

Acknowledge similarities without minimizing differences:

"I know we both loved Dad, and I know we both want to honor what he built, but in different ways. You want to carry it forward. I want to release it. Neither of us is wrong for how we feel, even if it's not what the other one wants to hear."

(Affirm the shared love, but also the divergent paths. No erasure. No moral high ground.)

Review the narrative accepted as fact:

"I've been telling myself that keeping the business means keeping a part of Dad alive. But when I slow down, I remember what he actually said: he wanted us to have *options,* and he wanted *happiness* to be our top priority. Holding onto something that drains me isn't what he wanted, nor is it what I want. And I think we've both been holding onto narratives that feel honorable but are actually making us stuck."

(Gently challenges the inherited story: that legacy means obligation, or that walking away is betrayal.)

Engage for conversation, not conversion:

"I'm not asking you to agree with me. I'm asking if we can talk with a neutral third party about what honoring Dad *looks like* now, not what it looked like then. What's true for *us,* today? I don't want to fight. I want to find clarity."

(You're not dragging her into your decision—you're offering a space where truth can breathe.)

Why This Matters:

In families, especially when legacy is involved, silence can feel like respect and guilt can masquerade as loyalty. D.A.R.E. helps you tell the truth *out loud, not* just in your group chats and therapy sessions.

Your father didn't build a business so you could burn yourself out trying to keep it alive. He built something out of love. And love requires honesty even when it leads to a hard choice.

5. The Uncle Whispers

Let's talk about a deeply sensitive topic. One that too many families whisper about, but rarely confront directly. One we cannot afford to handle lightly.

I am talking about inappropriate behavior, specifically sexual misconduct within families. It is not just uncomfortable to talk about, but traumatic and dangerous. And for too long, too many families and family members have stayed silent while a predator comfortably mingled in their midst. The silence has created comfort for the person who should be uncomfortable and left the burden on those who should be weightless. And for too many, it has become a generational curse, passed down in silence, secrets, and shame.

According to the U.S. Department of Justice, 34% of sexual abuse victims under the age of 18 are abused by family members. And a 2021 CDC report found that 1 in 4 girls and 1 in 13 boys in the U.S. experience sexual abuse at some point in childhood, most often by someone they know and trust.

This next scenario is not included for shock value. It's here because someone reading this has lived it or is trying to protect someone else from it.

Let's walk through what it might look like to apply the D.A.R.E. model to one of the most painful family dynamics: the known-but-ignored predator.

The Situation:

In your family, his name is Uncle Ray.

When you were younger, people told you to stay in groups, to never be alone in a room with him, and to sit on the far side of the couch. No one ever used the word "dangerous." They just said, "Just be careful around him, you know how he is." So you learned to manage the risk. Quietly. You'd scoot away when he came close. You'd hug but push away quickly during the customary family greeting. You'd make up a reason not to go when he asked, "Want to ride to the store with me?"

Now you're grown. You've been managing for decades, but it is a new day, and your little niece…you refuse to put her at risk. You thought you were fine, but you heard her get her first "watch out for Uncle Ray" warning, and you nearly lost it. To make matters worse, she just came and told you that Uncle Ray made a comment and put his hand on her lower back. She didn't feel safe. And now you have a choice.

D.A.R.E. Moment: Gathering the Family Elders and Decision-Makers

Describe vs. Interpret: "At the last gathering, my niece told me that Uncle Ray touched her in a way that made her uncomfortable. I want to be clear, this isn't the first time something like this has come up in our family. I received a warning about Uncle Ray when I was as young as five years old and not just from one person. At least four adults warned me. I am no longer going to remain silent or ask another generation to remain silent."

Acknowledge similarities without minimizing differences: "I know people love him. I know there are memories of better times. And I know this is painful to hear, especially when it's easier to pretend it's not that serious. But ignoring it doesn't make it go away nor lessen the severity. It just makes space for it to happen again."

Review the narrative accepted as fact: "For years, we've told the girls to stay away from him, to be careful. That was our 'plan.' But warnings are not protection. They're a cover-up. And that silence has allowed harm to continue under the excuse of family unity."

Engage for conversation not conversion: "I'm not here to make anyone comfortable; I am here to protect the children in our family and stop a pattern. I'm asking us to put real boundaries in place. He should not be around children. Period. And if that makes some people uncomfortable, so be it. We cannot keep sacrificing safety to protect a reputation. Silence is not protection. Let's engage in a productive conversation about how we protect this family's children and other children he may potentially encounter.

Why This Matters:

This is not about punishment. It's about prevention. It's about protecting the girls who are coming up now and refusing to pass down the culture of "we don't talk about that."

The D.A.R.E. Model doesn't fix this. This is bigger than one conversation, and in cases of abuse or suspected abuse, legal and therapeutic interventions are essential. D.A.R.E. is not a substitute for mandated reporting or law enforcement, but what D.A.R.E. *does* offer is a framework for finally saying the thing, clearly, courageously, and with full accountability.

Because love doesn't mean covering up harm, and silence is not a family value worth protecting.

You may lose some relationships by speaking up, but you will gain integrity, self-respect, and possibly the safety of someone who still has time to be protected.

Here's an additional section to follow the family confrontation using D.A.R.E.. This one is written with the same care, grounded tone, and clarity—designed for someone who *is* the niece, or anyone who has been made to feel unsafe by a family member but hasn't known how to speak up.

What If You're the Niece? What If You're the One It Happened To?

Let's be real: speaking up in families is hard. But speaking up about *this*? When the person is "known," loved, protected, maybe even powerful?

It can feel impossible. So if you're the niece or anyone in the position of being harmed or uncomfortable, you are not overreacting. You are not dramatic, and you are not alone. If something happened or *is* happening that made you feel unsafe, you don't need perfect words. But if you want a starting place, here's one way to use the D.A.R.E. model to speak your truth, with power and clarity.

D.A.R.E. Moment: Opening Dialogue with a Trusted Adult in the Family

Describe vs Interpret: "At the last gathering, Uncle Ray touched me in a way that didn't feel right. It made me uncomfortable, and I didn't know what to do in the moment, so I left it alone. But I don't feel okay staying silent about it."

Acknowledge similarities without minimizing differences: "I know this might be hard to hear. I know people love him or say, 'that's just how he is.' But that doesn't change how it made me feel, and it's not okay."

Review the narratives you have accepted as fact: "I think part of me assumed adults would notice. Or that if I just stayed away, it would solve the problem. But I don't want to keep avoiding family events just to feel safe. That's not fair to me."

Engage for conversation not conversion: "I'm telling you because I want this addressed. I don't want to be in spaces where people make excuses for behavior that harms others. I'm open to talking more about this, but I also need boundaries in place to protect me and my other cousins."

Why This Matters:

Your job is not to protect adults from discomfort. Your job is to protect *yourself, especially if the adults have failed you in the area of protection.*

And if you're reading this, wondering whether what happened was "bad enough" to bring up, let's be clear: If it made you feel violated, afraid, ashamed, or unsafe… that's enough.

D.A.R.E. is not just a model for mature conversations. It's a tool for reclaiming your voice, especially when it's been dismissed, ignored, or stolen.

And here's what else is true:

You deserve to be believed.

You deserve to be protected.

And you are not responsible for managing other people's guilt or grief.

Chapter 8 Recap: Using the Model in Relationships

Cliff Notes, Dethra-Styles

This chapter was personal. If you've ever argued over group texts, plotted an escape plan before the family reunion, or felt like you were the only one in your family willing to say the hard thing out loud, this one was for you.

Here's what we've learned (the hard way): Families are the original battlegrounds for communication breakdown, and we don't always handle it well. Instead, we dodge, explode, and vent to cousins instead of talking to the person. And when things finally come out, they don't come out—they *erupt*.

That's where D.A.R.E. comes in. This chapter showed us that even in the most intimate spaces where stakes are high and emotions are higher, we still need a framework to find our voice, stay grounded, and disrupt generational silence.

Because what you *don't* say in families still has power. And what you *do* say, if you say it with clarity and care, can change the story.

Key Takeaways:

- You can love your people *and* still need boundaries.

- You can forgive someone *and* still tell the truth about what happened.

- Silence might feel like peace, but it often comes at the cost of understanding—and healing.

- The messy conversations we avoid become the messy patterns our kids inherit.

D.A.R.E. gave us a tool to handle five of the most complicated family dynamics:

- Wills and inheritance (and the cousin who was cut out without explanation)

- The in-law feud turned police call

- Sibling conflict over the family business

- The uncle everyone whispers about—but no one confronts

We even gave a second path: what to say when *you* are the niece. The one who's still healing. Still angry. Still unsure if anyone would have your back if you finally told the truth.

And that's what D.A.R.E. does, it doesn't just offer *language,* it offers *courage.*

Why This Matters:

Because unresolved conflict doesn't disappear, it gets quiet. It goes underground. Then it resurfaces in bitterness, awkward holidays, and group chats full of side-eyes and sarcasm.

And most of all it gets passed down.

You want to shift your family culture? Start by shifting the way you talk and what you can talk about.

Describe what happened.

Acknowledge where you agree without being silent about where you disagree.

Review the story you and your family have accepted, especially if it's not working anymore.

Engage not to win, but to understand and be understood.

Because love without communication is just shared DNA. But love *with* communication? That's legacy.

Call to Action:

Before your next family gathering, group chat intervention, or call from the cousin you lowkey blocked:

- What have I been avoiding because it's uncomfortable?
- Am I protecting peace or just prolonging dysfunction?
- Have I mistaken silence for maturity when what we need is honesty?

Then D.A.R.E. your way through it. Not for drama. Not for dominance. But because cycles don't break themselves. And you just might be the one equipped enough to do it differently.

Chapter 9

Making D.A.R.E. a Way of Life

The Office Fridge and the Fight That Fixed Everything

No one remembers who started the note war.

At first, it was simple: a neatly printed sign above the fridge in the employee lounge of Evergreen Behavioral Health read, *"Please clean out your items every Friday. Unlabeled items will be thrown away."*

By week three, someone had scribbled, *"Whoever threw out my yogurt, we need to talk."* Underneath that, someone else replied, *"It expired in March. We're in July. Let it go."*

Passive aggression is practically a workplace sport, and in this department, it had Olympic-level energy. Team meetings were tight-lipped. Side-eyes were plentiful. Collaboration? Minimal.

And then one day, Dr. Lena Brooks, Director of Community Programs and surprise owner of the expired yogurt, decided she was tired. Not of the fridge drama, exactly, but of the quiet dysfunction it represented.

"You know what," she said during a Thursday meeting, "this yogurt situation is stupid. But it's also a symptom."

The team froze.

She pulled out a marker and wrote four words on the whiteboard:

Describe. Acknowledge. Review. Engage.

Lena had just come back from a professional development retreat where the D.A.R.E. Model had been introduced. And something had clicked. Not just for work but for life.

She described what she'd been observing in the office. Not just the fridge notes, but the subtle erosion of trust and willingness to speak up. She acknowledged how tension had built over time and how no one, herself included, wanted to be the one to "make it a thing," even though it was clearly "a thing." She reviewed how assumptions had taken the place of actual conversations: "they don't respect me," "she's always doing the most," "this place is toxic," and how those narratives had calcified into resentment. Then she engaged, *"I think we can do better. I want us to try."*

What followed wasn't magical. No violins played. No group hug. But someone *did* laugh. And someone else admitted that they'd been afraid to bring up a real issue for months. The dam cracked. And from there, the water flowed.

Three weeks later, they had a team charter. Two months later, one of the most cynical staffers volunteered to run their quarterly town hall. Six months later, Lena's teenage daughter used the D.A.R.E. Model at school to confront a group of girls bullying her best friend.

Lena didn't just use D.A.R.E. in that meeting. She **lived it**, at work, at home, and in her community. And when someone asked her why she cared so much about how people related to each other, she simply said:

"Because it's not just about conflict. It's about connection. And that's how culture gets built and problems get solved, one conversation at a time."

How to Build a Culture of Better Conversations in Your Workplace, Home, and Community

There's a myth that culture is something created at a retreat, defined in a mission statement, or declared in an all-hands meeting. But the truth is more straightforward yet trickier. Culture is built in the moments *between* the moments: the hallway chats, the texts left read but never responded to, the eyebrow raised during a Zoom meeting. It's in how we handle miscommunications, power dynamics, awkward silences, and uncomfortable truths.

And if you're serious about making D.A.R.E. a way of life, it starts in the everyday culture of how we communicate, especially when it's hard.

Why It Matters More Than Ever

According to a Gallup study, only 23% of employees globally report feeling "engaged" at work. Top contributors to disengagement are poor communication and a lack of trust in leadership. Meanwhile, a *Harvard Business Review* article revealed that 69% of managers say they're uncomfortable communicating with employees, especially around performance or conflict.

That's not just a workplace problem, it's a people problem. And the ripple effect extends to our homes and communities. A Pew Research Center survey found that 61% of Americans say it's stressful to have political conversations with close friends or family. Add in race, gender, money, religion, or generational dynamics, and it's no wonder we default to silence, siloing, sarcasm, or snapping.

We weren't taught how to talk when it matters most.

The D.A.R.E. Model doesn't fix everything, but it gives people a way *in*. And that's how culture changes: not through big gestures, but through small, repeated patterns that feel safe, build trust, and create momentum.

Let's break down how to start building that culture, wherever you are.

In the Workplace: From "Professional" Silence to Productive Dialogue

We've been taught to "be professional," which often gets translated as "don't say anything that might make someone uncomfortable." But discomfort isn't the enemy; disrespect is. And when we avoid honest conversations to keep things comfortable, we breed the very dysfunction we're afraid of.

To create a culture of better conversations at work:

- **Model the model.** Leaders, listen up: culture cascades from the top. If you **describe** behaviors clearly without personal attacks, **acknowledge** others' perspectives openly, **review** your assumptions out loud, and **engage** to understand (not just to be right), your team will notice and mirror it.

- **Make conversations part of performance.** What if every performance review included a self-reflection question like, "Tell me about a time you used D.A.R.E. to handle a tough conversation?"

Now we're not just talking about results—we're evaluating the relational health that drives those results.

- **Normalize check-ins that go deeper.** During weekly standups, add one question: "Is there a conversation I've been avoiding that would help me move forward this week?" Just asking the question builds awareness and rewards people for tackling, not tiptoeing.

And please, stop outsourcing culture to HR. Every person who has a conversation contributes to the culture. You don't need a title to shape it. You need intention.

At Home: The Conversations That Shape Identity

Here's a hard truth: many of us were raised in homes where love was present but communication was conditional.

"Don't talk back."

"Because I said so."

"Let's not bring that up in front of your father."

If this sounds familiar, you're not alone. According to a study published in the *Journal of Family Issues*, over 64% of adults report growing up in households where open emotional expression was discouraged, especially around topics like disagreement, mental health, or family conflict. In many families, silence was a form of survival. However, that silence has had and continues to have consequences.

We can't build cultures of better conversations in the world if our own homes are steeped in avoidance, performance, or shame. That's why D.A.R.E. at home doesn't just help; it heals.

At home, D.A.R.E. works just as powerfully.

Describe, don't diagnose. Instead of saying, "You're always on that phone," try, "I've noticed we haven't had a deep conversation this week." One opens the door; the other slams it shut.

Data supports this finding: The Gottman Institute, renowned for its research on relationships, found that how conversations *start* predicts their outcome **96% of the time**. Conversations that begin with blame or contempt often end in shutdown. But those who begin with observation and curiosity are more likely to create connection.

Acknowledge their world, even if it's foreign to you. Your teenager might be crying over a social media breakup with a person they never met face-to-face. It's not about whether *you* get it; it's about whether *they* feel understood by you.

Research from Common Sense Media indicates that **75% of teens** report feeling more comfortable sharing their genuine feelings through text or social media than in person. That means parents and caregivers need to work harder to bridge the gap, *not dismiss it.*

When we acknowledge, we signal safety. And safety is where trust grows.

Review the stories you inherited. Are you parenting based on what healed you, or what hurt you? Are you trying to control outcomes because no one ever gave *you* space to question things?

These are D.A.R.E. moments, too; they are just happening as internal communication with yourself.

Intergenerational studies from the University of Minnesota show that communication patterns in childhood predict adult relational health and emotional regulation with nearly 80% accuracy. Translation? How you talk (or don't talk) at home shapes how your kids will relate, lead, and listen as adults.

Engage regularly, not reactively. If the only time your family talks about feelings is when there's yelling or crying, that's not culture, it's crisis management.

Set up regular "D.A.R.E. dinners," Sunday check-ins, or "say something real" moments. Even a five-minute walk after dinner, where the only rule is "we don't talk about logistics," can shift your entire home dynamic.

A study by the Family Dinner Project found that families who eat together at least three times a week report significantly higher rates of emotional well-being, school performance, and resilience in children, and lower rates of depression and substance use. The secret isn't in the food. It's in the *talking while chewing.*

Remember: what feels awkward at first becomes normal later. And what's normal in your home becomes the emotional blueprint for the next generation.

You're not just building a culture, you're breaking (or reinforcing) cycles.

In the Community: From Call-Out to Call-In

We're living in a time of cancel culture and confrontation. Social media has turned every disagreement into a performance, and nuance is often the first casualty. But change doesn't come from screaming into the void (or your phone screen). It comes from meaningful engagement with people we might disagree with, and that starts in our communities.

Whether it's your neighborhood association, your church group, your kid's school board, or your group chat from undergrad, here's how to build a better conversational culture in the community:

- **Be the invitation.** If there's tension in your group, don't wait for someone else to name it. Start with "Can I describe something I've been noticing?" That's D.A.R.E. in action, and leadership without the title.

- **Create structures that invite honesty.** Anonymous surveys, listening circles, and even group agreements about how you'll engage during tough topics all set the tone. One group I worked with added a D.A.R.E. anchor question to every meeting: "Have we created space for honest dialogue today?" Game changer.

- **Celebrate attempts, not just outcomes.** Someone tried to acknowledge a racial tension awkwardly? Say thank you, not "you could've said that better." Perfect conversations don't build culture, *brave ones* do.

- **Stay long enough to make it better.** Too often, we ghost communities when things get hard. But staying, engaging, and practicing D.A.R.E. isn't about comfort; it's about courage. Better conversations start when someone decides not to leave, not to lash out, but to lean in.

Making It Stick: The Culture Equation

Think of culture like compound interest. One honest conversation doesn't seem like much, but stacked daily over time, it transforms everything. Here's a simple framework:

Clarity + Consistency + Curiosity = Culture

- **Clarity:** Use D.A.R.E. to create language around effective communication. Define what "good conversations" look like

- **Consistency:** Practice even when it's hard. Especially when it's hard.

- **Curiosity:** Stay open. Ask, "What am I missing?" "What are they trying to say?" "What if I'm wrong?"

Together, these create a culture where people aren't just allowed to speak, speaking up is expected, they are equipped to be successful, and supported even when they don't get it perfect or others disagree.

You Are the Culture

Here's what most people forget: *you are always building culture.* Whether by default or design, whether through action or avoidance, whether through D.A.R.E. or dysfunction, you are shaping how people experience communication around you.

So the real question isn't "How do I build a culture of better conversations?"

The real question is: "What kind of culture is my silence, sarcasm, or sincerity building right now?"

Better conversations aren't just a skillset. They're a lifestyle. And the D.A.R.E. Model isn't a formula to memorize, it's a mindset to embody. At work, at home, and in the world.

The Mindset Shift: From Conflict Avoidance to Productive Engagement

What I have learned in my over …years (those… are on purpose. It

215

means a lot, and you don't need to know the exact number of years) is that most of us were not raised to handle conflict well.

We were raised to:

- Change the subject
- Swallow our feelings
- Write *extremely detailed* texts that never get sent
- And, in more advanced households, weaponize our nonverbals from facial expressions to audible sighs

Conflict avoidance is a full-time job. It's exhausting. And the pay is horrible. Here's the good news: it wasn't your fault. You were socialized this way. But if you continue this way, it is your fault because we have tools to change this. We just spent an entire book together working this out.

A study published in *Personality and Individual Differences* found that 70% of people admit they avoid conflict because they "don't want to make things worse," and 62% say they "don't know what to say" when things get tense.

Translation? Most people would rather stay uncomfortable forever than risk five minutes of discomfort.

We've confused silence with peace, avoidance with maturity, and "letting it go" with actually being okay.

Let's fix that.

You Don't Hate Conflict, You Hate *Bad* Conflict

First, let's make one thing clear: you're not conflict-averse. You just hate the kind of conflict that feels like a courtroom, a Twitter thread, or Thanksgiving at your auntie's house after someone says "not all men."

What you hate is:

- Feeling misunderstood
- Losing control
- Being disrespected
- Or, maybe most of all, being wrong publicly

216

We don't fear conflict. We fear *unproductive* conflict because most of what we've seen has been ugly. We weren't taught how to do it well, and it shows.

But productive conflict? That's not scary. That's where change happens. That's where ideas get better. That's where relationships deepen. That's where clarity lives.

Productive conflict is just *disagreement with dignity.*

The Workplace: Where Conflict Goes to Die (Quietly, Passive-Aggressively, and in Slack Threads)

If you've ever been in a meeting where everyone agrees out loud and immediately complains in a group chat, you already know where this is going– we are masters at fake agreement.

According to a report from Fierce, Inc., 80% of employees are currently holding onto unspoken concerns at work, usually because they're afraid of how speaking up will be received. That's 8 out of 10 people silently stewing through PowerPoints and performance reviews.

And when employees do speak up, research from MIT Sloan shows that leaders are 32% more likely to reward silence than they are to reward healthy dissent.

So what do people do?

They perform politeness. They say, "Great idea!" when they mean, "That will definitely backfire." They nod. They smile. And then they send résumés to other companies that might listen.

Conflict Avoidance Has a Cost

Let's be clear: avoiding conflict is *not* a neutral act. It's a form of quiet sabotage of relationships, progress, and peace of mind.

Here's what conflict avoidance costs you:

- **At work:** Innovation stalls, resentment festers, and performance tanks. One Harvard Business School study found that unresolved conflicts cost U.S. businesses $359 billion annually in lost productivity.

- **At home:** Connection fades. Misunderstandings deepen. One partner's inner monologue becomes a full-on novella. (Spoiler alert: you're the villain.)

- **In your community:** Tough conversations get skipped. Problems go underground. People only communicate in echo chambers of like-minded individuals.

In short, the conversation you avoid doesn't go away; it just goes somewhere else, usually a deeper, darker, and more harmful place.

Rebranding Conflict: From Fight to Fix

Part of the problem is language. Think about the words we use:

- "Address the issue"

- "Call them out"

- "Put them in their place"

These are not the phrases of a healthy conversational culture. These are wrestling promos.

But what if we reframed conflict as a **conversation with stakes**? Not a battle, but a bridge. Not a win/lose, but a *reveal* of truth, tension, or opportunity.

That's the mindset shift.

And here's the truth bomb: Conflict isn't what breaks relationships. Poorly handled conflict does.

D.A.R.E. and the Mindset Shift: From "I Can't Say That" to "Here's How I'll Say It"

The D.A.R.E. Model flips the script on conflict.

It takes you from:

- "I'm not trying to start anything." to "Let me describe what I noticed."

- "I don't want to argue" to "I want to acknowledge how this might land for you."

- "They're just being difficult." to "Let me review the story I'm telling myself about their behavior."

- "They don't deserve a response" to "I'm going to engage; not to change them, but to represent myself well."

That's power, sustainable power.

And most of us have never seen it modeled.

Conversational Competence Is a Muscle, Not a Trait

One of the biggest lies we believe is that some people are just "naturally good" at conflict. You know, the smooth talkers. The ones who can diffuse any situation.

But handling conflict well is not a personality trait. It's a skill. And like any skill, it improves with practice.

Studies on conversational training show that after just two hours of focused dialogue practice, people report a 46% increase in confidence navigating high-stakes conversations.

The key is reps. You don't get good at conflict by thinking about it. You get good at conflict by *having more of it* in better, braver ways.

Fun with Avoidance: Are You a Ninja, a Ghost, or a Saboteur?

Let's lighten it up. Here are a few classic conflict-avoidance archetypes. Recognize yourself?

The Ninja – Master of stealth at avoiding the moment. Disappears the moment tension enters the room. Leaves group chats quietly. Slips out of conversations without a trace. Hopes the problem evaporates if it's never mentioned and moves in silence like it never happened.

The Ghost – Doesn't just exit the conversation, they disappear from the whole relationship and avoid everything related to the people involved. Will vanish instead of replying to an uncomfortable email. Avoids eye contact at work. Comes back three weeks later and says, "Just seeing this!" Lies. They saw it, they didn't want to deal with it or you..

The Saboteur – Seems fine on the surface. Says "no worries!" but sends screenshots to their best friend, takes notes, and holds grudges. Their resentment simmers, and eventually, they *will* get even. They pretend externally but plot internally.

The Performer – Puts on a show for peace. Says "it's all good" while quietly falling apart inside. They're not scheming or escaping—they're just exhausted from pretending everything's fine when it's not. They pretend externally while breaking internally.

If you see yourself in any of these, don't worry, you're in good company. Most of us were trained in one of these styles. But now, we train for something better.

The New Mindset Mantra: Clarity Over Comfort

When people ask me the secret to shifting from conflict avoidance to productive engagement, I give them this: **"Don't aim to be comfortable. Aim to be clear."**

Comfort is temporary. Clarity is sustainable.

Comfort is silent. Clarity speaks.

Comfort suppresses. Clarity reveals.

Comfort walks away saying, "Whatever." Clarity stands there and says, "Help me understand."

When You Shift…

Here's the beautiful part: once you start showing up differently in conflict, other people often rise with you.

You:

- Lower your voice, they stop yelling

- Ask a real question, they give a real answer

- Own your part, they stop defending theirs

Not always. Not instantly. But often enough to be worth it. And even when they don't, you win because you stayed aligned with your values, and you modeled what peace looks like with a spine.

That's the shift.

Challenge: Take the Leap, Not the L

Here's your mindset shift moment. Think of a conversation you've been avoiding. That one.

Now ask yourself:

- What am I afraid will happen?

- What might happen if it goes *well?*

- Who do I become if I choose clarity over comfort?

You don't need to be fearless. Just willing.

Conflict isn't a detour; it's the work. And the better you get at it, the lighter life feels.

No more dodging. No more disappearing. No more losing sleep over things that could be cleared up with one intentional, honest, D.A.R.E.-style conversation.

From now on, it's clarity over comfort, it's engagement over avoidance, it's you—living free, and talking like it.

When D.A.R.E. Doesn't Work: There's Always One

Danielle knew better. She *knew* better.

She was at her friend Bria's annual "We Survived the School Year" cook-out—a festive, shady-backyard, plastic-chair and red Solo cup situation full of people who had mastered the art of small talk, spades, and suspicious side-eyes at unfamiliar dishes. You know the type of gathering with loud music, too many cars parked in front of the house, and more guests than you remember inviting.

Danielle was having a lovely time, sipping "lemonade" (quotation marks very intentional) and minding her business, when someone tapped her shoulder.

"You work in DEI, right?" the man asked.

He was wearing cargo shorts, a backwards cap, and the confident smile of a man who just knew he was about to say something profound.

"Sort of," she replied, already bracing herself. "I work in organizational strategy, and DEI is a part of that."

He nodded like he'd just confirmed she worked for the Illuminati.

"Well, I've been thinking, I don't believe in all this identity politics stuff. I mean, shouldn't we all just be human? I treat everybody the same."

Danielle smiled politely. She'd heard this before. It was a classic that seemed to stay on repeat in the minds and mouths of too many people who misunderstood DEI like it was their job to do so.

Still, she decided to give him a shot.

- **Describe vs Interpret**: "It sounds like you're saying you value treating people with fairness. I hear that."

- **Acknowledge similarities without minimizing differences**: "I think most people do want to be treated well. And it makes sense that you'd want things to feel equal."

- **Review the narrative you have accepted as fact**: "That said, I'm noticing a pattern where people equate treating everyone the same with treating everyone equitably, which can actually miss the fact that not everyone has the same needs. Would you help a man in a wheelchair onto a curb the same way you would help a pregnant woman? "

She paused, watched him, and waited.

He squinted at her like she'd started speaking ancient Greek.

"So what, we're supposed to hand out trophies for oppression now?"

Ah.

There it was.

Obstinance. Party of one. Table's ready.

She gave it one more try.

- **Engage for conversation not conversion**: "I love this topic and would enjoy an exchange of ideas, even if they're different. Tell me, what do you know about DEI?"

He blinked.

"Oh, I'm just saying, everybody's too sensitive nowadays. Life was better when women stayed home with the kids and men could be men. Ain't no DEI gone change my mind about that."

Bingo.

That was Danielle's cue to lean in, not to argue, but to confirm what she suspected. She asked gently:

"So, did you come to converse about this topic, or to convince me I'm doing work that's not worth doing?"

He blinked again.

"Well, it shouldn't even be a job."

She tilted her head. "Are you open to exchanging ideas?"

"There are no ideas to exchange. DEI is some BS pulled out of the crack of liberals' butt, and it's ruining our country."

And there it was. The final buzzer. Game over.

Danielle smiled, raised her cup slightly, and said:

"Got it. Alright then, I'm gonna go check on that potato salad. Good talk."

And she meant it.

She walked away mid-conversation, without guilt, without sarcasm, and without engaging in a back-and-forth that would've just become a TED Talk for an audience of one who wasn't listening.

She didn't storm off. She didn't flip a table. She didn't try to prove she was smarter, more evolved, or better-read on systemic inequity.

She just… exited.

Later, someone asked her, "Weren't you talking to Marcus?"

She nodded. "Briefly. But I could tell we weren't having a conversation, we were about to have a standoff disguised as dialogue, and I wasn't interested. I D.A.R.E.'d it and then I exited."

Exit Is Not Failure. It's Fluency.

Danielle didn't back down. She didn't run. She didn't default to "just let it go."

She engaged with intention. She used the model:

- **Describe** the dynamic.
- **Acknowledge** the perspective.
- **Review** the assumptions.
- **Engage** with clarity and an open invitation.

And then she made the most strategic move available: she stopped talking.

Because sometimes, walking away is not an act of surrender, it's an act of self-respect and peace maintenance.

D.A.R.E. isn't about dragging yourself through a dialogue with someone who's already told you through their tone, their tactics, or their tantrum that they don't want a conversation. They want control, or a soapbox, or an audience.

Danielle didn't give him any of those things, and that wasn't rudeness. That was **fluency**. The D.A.R.E. model had done its job—not by changing him, but by guiding her decision-making.

She gave him the gift of her exit. And she gave herself the gift of her peace.

What People Get Wrong About D.A.R.E.

When people say "D.A.R.E. didn't work," here's what they usually mean:

- "The other person didn't agree with me."

- "They got defensive anyway."
- "They didn't suddenly become more emotionally mature."
- "It still felt uncomfortable."

Let's fix that right now: D.A.R.E. is not a spell. It doesn't force people into growth.

It's a clarity tool. It helps you make sound communication decisions in the middle of messy human dynamics.

That's its superpower, not perfection, but precision.

D.A.R.E. helps you:

- Communicate what's real.
- Stay grounded in your values.
- Name the thing without igniting the flames.
- Know when enough has been said.

That's *still* winning even if they're still wrong.

The Dual Purpose of D.A.R.E.

We said this earlier, but let's say it louder:

D.A.R.E. has two jobs.

1. To help you *navigate* the conversation toward a productive end.
2. To help you *identify* when the conversation is becoming inefficient and unproductive.

Most people only expect the first. They assume D.A.R.E. means "hang in there." But sometimes, the most potent part of the model is the moment you realize:

"Oh, this isn't a conversation. This is a lecture. A performance. A trap. A loop. A black hole of ego. And I'm done participating."

D.A.R.E. doesn't just help you *enter* a conversation well. It enables you to **exit** one *wisely*.

The Hotel Exit Analogy

Think of it like a hotel.

When you check in, what's one of the first things they want you to know? Not where the snacks are. Not how to operate the remote. They display emergency exit signs in large, bold letters.

Because safety is more important than scenery.

Even if you never need them, those exits are designed into the building—clearly marked, lit in the dark, accessible no matter your condition.

That's how the D.A.R.E. Model is built. Yes, it helps you settle in, get comfortable, and communicate well. But it also makes sure you know where the exits are *in case of fire*.

Sometimes the safest place is *outside the conversation.*

And D.A.R.E. keeps you safe whether you stay or whether you go.

What Does "Go" Look Like?

Let's talk about the *go*.

Because *"go"* doesn't always mean dramatic walkouts or slamming car doors.

In Danielle's case, *go* meant leaving the conversation entirely. Not because she was scared. Not because she couldn't hold her own. But because Marcus wasn't there to talk, he was there to tussle.

He wanted a platform, not a perspective. He wanted to argue, not exchange. And she realized—brilliantly, by the way—that there was nothing to be gained but a headache and a story for the group chat.

So she left. Not with hostility. With clarity. She had already D.A.R.E.'d the conversation to its limit. And when she saw there was no reciprocity, no curiosity, and no growth ahead, she took the nearest exit. That's not quitting, that's wisdom with legs.

But in other cases, *go* doesn't mean permanent; it means *pause.*

Sometimes you go because:

- You need to cool off before you say something you can't unsay.

- You need to gather your thoughts so you're not word-vomiting emotion.

- You need to gather information because you realize you don't need a conversation; you need a class (we will revisit this in a minute).

- You need to go get help from a supervisor, mediator, a mentor, a therapist, or someone who can help you navigate what's next.

- You realize the conversation is above your training or pay grade.

Go might look like saying:

- "Let's revisit this after we've both had some time to think."

- "I want to keep talking, but I need to check a few things first."

- "I'm open to re-engaging, but not in this tone or energy."

In those cases, *go* is temporary, strategic, and rooted in your long-term peace, not your short-term pride.

The point is this: D.A.R.E. gives you the language to stay grounded *and* the insight to know when grounded isn't good enough, and you need to leave.

You Don't Have to Say It All to Say Enough

Sometimes we avoid ending a conversation because we haven't "said everything."

Here's a hard truth: you don't need to say everything. You just need to say *enough* to gain the clarity you need.

Clarity is the finish line, not their agreement.

Ask yourself:

- Do I understand where they're coming from, even if I disagree?

- Have I said what I needed to say?

- Will any more words lead to more truth or just more tension?

- If the answers are yes, yes, and no?

Then, close the laptop. Put down the phone. Say, "Alright then," and log out of the drama.

D.A.R.E. didn't fail. It *freed you*.

Knowing When Not to Speak at All

Let me say this clearly: Not every conversation deserves your effort.

Sometimes:

- You've already done your part.

- The other person isn't emotionally available or mature.

- You're too tired to do this again.

- It's not the right moment.

- The relationship is better served by boundaries, not words.

- OR, it's not that serious

That's not avoidance. That's discernment.

D.A.R.E. doesn't mean "force every issue." It means, "decide with intention what needs to be said and what doesn't." You don't need to D.A.R.E. the conversation with someone who mistakenly backed their grocery cart into you at the grocery store. You need to accept their apology, even if it was only a half-apology, and head to the produce section.

The goal is to engage when it's worth it, and to exit when it's wise.

Class, Not Conversation

Have you ever been in a conversation thinking you were an expert? Expert may be a stretch, but you felt like you knew what you were talking about, and midway in the conversatio,n there was a revelation, and just like that, it hit you:

"Oh no, there is a lot more I need to know to engage with these people."

You realized you did not need a conversation; you needed a class. You needed to learn a lot more about the topic at hand before you engaged in any kind of debate or disagreement.

This is not a failure; this is a sign of **growth.**

There are moments when the most D.A.R.E.-ful thing you can do is recognize that you don't need a comeback, a debate, or even a conversation. What you need is to learn; you need a **class.**

Sometimes it sneaks up on you.

You start sharing your opinion on a topic, and then someone across from you brings depth, nuance, data, or lived experience you didn't know about, hadn't heard about, or even considered. And suddenly, you shift from "let me tell you what I think" to "tell me more about that."

If your ego is too loud, you'll keep talking, grasping for solid ground, hoping no one notices that your facts are wobbly and your arguments are not sound.

But if you have used D.A.R.E. up to this point, turning the conversation into a class is easy. You can easily pause, listen, and pivot.

How D.A.R.E. Helps You Course-Correct Without Shame

The beauty of D.A.R.E. is that it doesn't just help you stay in a conversation. It enables you to know when to shift *how* you're in it.

Here's how D.A.R.E. can support this pivot:

- **Describe** what's happening:

  "I'm realizing in real time that I don't know as much about this as I thought I did."

- **Acknowledge** what the other person is offering:

  "You've spent time with this topic. I appreciate you sharing—it's opening my eyes."

- **Review** your role in the moment:

  "I thought I was ready to contribute, but what I need to do is listen and learn."

- **Engage** with curiosity, not commentary:

  "Do you have any resources you'd recommend so I can go deeper before I come back to this conversation?"

No defensiveness and no faking it. Just humility and presence. That's not weakness, it's wisdom.

The Positive Outcome of Owning Your Learning Curve

When you acknowledge you need a class, not a conversation, several good things happen:

- You take the pressure off yourself to be the expert.

- You give the other person space to feel heard and valued.

- You model emotional maturity for everyone in earshot.

- You prevent a performative, unproductive back-and-forth.

- You grow.

And a bonus? You build your reputation as a person who will converse for understanding, not conversion or "the win."

That's the kind of conversational partner people trust. That's the kind of leadership we need more of.

The Real Win: You Grew

Let's bring it full circle.

When D.A.R.E. "doesn't work" because the other person shuts down, gets loud, deflects, or becomes a human firewall—or because you recognized the need to pause and learn—you didn't fail.

You:

- Used a model to stay grounded.

- Practiced emotional maturity and discernment.

- Choose curiosity over control.

- Modeled what genuine dialogue *could* look like.

That's a win.

Because you can't control the outcome, but you can *own your approach.*

And every time you use the model, whether it ends in breakthrough or boundaries, you grow.

You flex your conversational competence. You build trust with yourself. You get better at how to enter, navigate, and exit without self-betrayal.

And that, my friend, is fluency.

Final Thoughts: The Conversations You're Avoiding Might Be the Ones That Change Everything

You didn't pick up this book because you were bored and wanted to alphabetize your self-help collection.

You picked it up because **there's a conversation.** A real one. A big one.

The one that's been sitting in the pit of your stomach, riding shotgun in your thoughts, showing up in your dreams wearing a name tag that says, *"Hey, it's me. That thing you don't want to deal with."*

You know precisely which conversation I'm talking about. Maybe it's the one with your partner where you finally tell the truth about how distant things feel. Or the one with your boss, where you ask for what you want or establish some boundaries that are long overdue. Maybe it's the one with your sibling, or your best friend, or your parent, where you stop pretending everything's fine and finally say what needs to be said.

You picked up this book because you were tired of holding it in. Tired of swallowing the words. Tired of wondering what might happen if you just said the thing. And you knew the only thing stopping you from saying "the thing" was your incompetence, conversational incompetence to be exact. You know you struggled to engage in conversations where there is a high likelihood of disagreement.

Let me tell you what happens when you say this thing: **everything changes.**

Not always perfectly. Not always painlessly. But always powerfully. And the outcome you get is determined by the methods you use.

You've Learned the Model. Now It's Time to Use It.

Over the last few chapters, you've laughed (hopefully), thought deeply (definitely), and maybe even had a few lightbulb moments where you went, "Ohhh, that's why that conversation didn't go so well."

Let's remind you what you've got in your back pocket now:

- **Describe** instead of interpret. Stick to the facts and not your feelings about the facts. There is a time for your feelings, but right now we need Black and white.

- **Acknowledge** similarities without minimizing differences or pretending to agree. You don't have to co-sign to show you heard

- **Review** the narratives—yours, theirs, and the ones you both inherited that might be shaping the tension.

- **Engage** for clarity, not conversion. This isn't a battle to win, it's a bridge to build.

You've seen how D.A.R.E. works at work. You've seen how it works in families. You've seen how it protects your peace, strengthens your relationships, and helps you walk away when walking away is what's wise.

You're ready.

But What If I'm Still Scared?

You might be. That's fine. Courage is not the absence of fear; it's the decision that your growth is more important than your comfort.

Here is the truth, the reality that you have to accept: you are already in discomfort.

The conversation you won't have has you STRESSED OUT!

You know the stress of avoiding the conversation. You know the mental gymnastics of pretending everything's fine. You know the imaginary arguments in the shower, the carefully crafted text messages that never get sent, the fake smiles you flash in rooms where your silence is eating you alive.

You are already in discomfort.

But do you know what's on the other side of that conversation?

Maybe it's healing. Maybe it's closure. Maybe it's a boundary. Maybe it's the beginning of something new.

Or maybe it's just peace.

But you'll never know unless you D.A.R.E..

The D.A.R.E. D.A.R.E.

Here's your challenge. Your triple-dog-D.A.R.E., if you will. Pick the conversation. You know the one.

Use the model even if it's messy, even if you fumble, even if your voice shakes. (Heck, especially if your voice shakes.)

Use the model with your team, your kids, and your partner. That coworker who's one "per my last email" away from getting blocked in real life.

Let this book be more than notes and underlines, and highlighted quotes. Let it be a launchpad.

If you want extra credit and to see improvements in the life of those around you, don't stop at the triple-dog-D.A.R.E.. Don't just use D.A.R.E.; spread it. The world doesn't need more people who know how to argue. It needs more people who know how to engage.

So here's what you do next:

1. **Use the model.** You've got the tools. Start the conversation. It is a muscle; you first must start using it, then strengthen it.

2. **Share the model.** Teach it to your teams, your friends, your family, your loud cousin at Thanksgiving.

3. **Bring D.A.R.E. training to your organization and leadership.** Because when leaders are trained and held accountable, communication improves, trust deepens, and culture transforms. D.A.R.E. training today means a better workplace tomorrow.

4. **Share the book.** Buy a copy for the people in your life–work and home– who need it. You know who they are (Yes, *them.*). But only after you read it.

Final Words (But Not the End)

This isn't goodbye. One of my favorite songs in Hamilton is "One Last Time", it is the song where Washington lays out for Hamilton how they prevent having an aristocracy in the newly founded country. He tells Hamilton they have to teach the people how to say goodbye because their inclination will be to become dependent on a person, and that person becomes king.

My favorite lines are:

One last time

And if we get this right

We're gonna teach 'em how to say

Goodbye

If I say goodbye, the nation learns to move on

It outlives me when I'm gone.

That was why I wrote this book. I deliver keynotes and workshops around the world, I coach executives at the highest level, and at the end, everyone asks, "How do we keep a small piece of you with us?" At each event, I have to say "goodbye," but what you learned doesn't.

This is your new beginning.

Because once you learn how to D.A.R.E., you'll never unlearn it.

You'll never go back to ghosting instead of talking. You'll never settle for simmering instead of saying. You'll never confuse silence for peace again, and the legacy of the knowledge will outlive us both.

So go. Have the conversation. It might feel scary. But it might also set you free.

D.A.R.E. to find out.

TLTR
Too Long To Read

Born from the internet's favorite shortcut, TLTR (Too Long To Read) is a playful spin on the OG "TL;DR" (Too Long; Didn't Read), which started in online forums and Reddit threads where people wrote novels and readers begged for the SparkNotes. Over time, TLDR became the go-to for getting the gist without the deep dive.

This is that, but better.

Each chapter in this book comes with a TLTR: a quick, smart, and slightly spicy summary of the key ideas. It's not a replacement for the whole chapter, but it's a solid snack to hold you over until you can come back and eat the entire meal. Whether you missed a section, need a refresher, or just want the cliff notes before a tough conversation, this section has your back.

Let's be honest: life gets busy. TLTR is how we stay ready.

Chapter 1: We Need to Talk, But We Don't Know How

Proverbs 18:13 (NIV)

"To answer before listening—that is folly and shame."

Hard conversations don't have to be harmful. In this opening chapter, we meet Marissa, someone trying to say the right thing, the right way, at the right time (and realizing that's harder than it looks). We explore why difficult conversations often go sideways and introduce the idea that communication is a skill, not a personality trait. The good news? You can learn it. And when you do, you'll unlock better outcomes, stronger relationships, and a lot more peace of mind.

Chapter 2: What Is Conversational Competence?

Colossians 4:6 (NIV)

"Let your conversation be always full of grace, seasoned with salt, so that you may know how to answer everyone."

You know how to talk, but do you know how to talk *through* conflict? This chapter introduces conversational competence as the key to handling tough topics with clarity, empathy, and confidence. You'll get a first look at the **D.A.R.E. Model**, learn what gets in the way of healthy dialogue, and take a quiz to assess your current conflict style. It's not about perfection, it's about progress. And this is where it starts.

Chapter 3: Describe vs. Interpret-Facts, Feelings, and Fiction

Proverbs 18:17 (NIV)

"In a lawsuit the first to speak seems right, until someone comes forward and cross-examines."

Before you can fix a conversation, you have to understand what actually happened. In this chapter, we dig into the first step of the **D.A.R.E. Model: Describe vs Interpret**. You'll learn how to separate observations from assumptions, facts from feelings, and how to open a conversation with clarity instead of confusion. This simple (but powerful) shift sets the tone for resolution, not reaction, and helps everyone feel like they're playing the same game on the same field.

Chapter 4: Acknowledge — The Balance Between Finding Common Ground and Respecting Differences

Romans 12:18 (NIV)

"If it is possible, as far as it depends on you, live at peace with everyone."

When people feel seen and heard, everything shifts. In this chapter, we explore the second step of the **D.A.R.E. Model: Acknowledge similarities without minimizing differences**. You'll learn how to honor someone's perspective without needing to agree, and how to build stronger connections by recognizing both what unites us *and* what makes us different. Using a workplace story that's all too relatable, we show how acknowledgment creates psychological safety, deepens trust, and keeps conversations moving forward—even when topics get tense.

Chapter 5: Review — The Narrative(s) You Have Accepted as Fact

Psalm 139:23–24 (NIV)

"Search me, God, and know my heart; test me and know my anxious thoughts. See if there is any offensive way in me, and lead me in the way everlasting."

Your brain is a brilliant storyteller, and sometimes, it's a little *too* convincing. This chapter invites you into the third step of the **D.A.R.E. Model**: **Review the narrative you have accepted as fact**. You'll learn how to examine the stories you've been telling yourself about people, power, and performance, and discover how those narratives shape your communication. With the right tools, you can challenge old assumptions, make room for new possibilities, and approach conversations with curiosity instead of conclusion. This is where clarity, growth, and better outcomes begin.

Chapter 6: Engage for Conversation, Not Conversion

James 1:19 (NIV)

"Everyone should be quick to listen, slow to speak and slow to become angry."

Every great conversation starts with a simple mindset shift: connection over convincing. This chapter dives into the final step of the **D.A.R.E. Model**: **Engage for conversation, not conversion**. You'll learn how to show up ready to *listen*, not just respond, and how to participate in dialogue that builds trust, even when you don't agree. Engaging well means letting go of the need to "win" and focusing instead on clarity, curiosity, and mutual respect. The goal isn't to convert; it is to connect, understand, and get to a mutually beneficial resolution.

Chapter 7: Conversational Competence Is a Leadership Skill

Proverbs 15:1 (NIV)

> *"A gentle answer turns away wrath, but a harsh word stirs up anger."*

Leadership isn't just about vision; it's about communication. In this chapter, we connect the dots between conversational competence and effective leadership. Whether you're managing a team, running a household, or leading from the middle, your ability to navigate conflict, foster clarity, and build trust is what sets you apart. You'll see how the **D.A.R.E. Model** boosts performance, strengthens relationships, and equips you to lead with confidence even in the messy, high-stakes moments.

Chapter 8: From Tension to Truth-Using the D.A.R.E. Model to Strengthen Love, Family, and Friendship

Ephesians 4:2–3 (NIV)

> *"Be completely humble and gentle; be patient, bearing with one another in love. Make every effort to keep the unity of the Spirit through the bond of peace."*

Real relationships come with real emotions and sometimes, real tension. This chapter shows how the **D.A.R.E. Model** helps you move from awkward silence or simmering frustration to honest, productive connection. Whether you're navigating parenting, partnership, or that one friend who always "means well," you'll learn how to approach conversations with love, clarity, and courage. Vulnerability becomes a strength. Differences become invitations. And communication becomes the bridge that keeps your most essential relationships strong, even when things get hard.

Chapter 9: Making D.A.R.E. a Way of Life

Micah 6:8 (NIV)

> *"He has shown you, O mortal, what is good. And what does the Lord require of you? To act justly and to love mercy and to walk humbly with your God."*

This final chapter is your launchpad. It's where the **D.A.R.E. Model** moves from something you *learned* to something you *live*. Through real-world examples—from workplace yogurt wars to family tension and back-yard debates—you'll see how **Describe, Acknowledge, Review, and Engage** show up in everyday life. You'll learn how to build a culture of better communication at work, at home, and in your community—and how to exit a conversation when needed, without guilt. Most importantly, you'll walk away with the courage to stop avoiding the conversations that matter and start using your voice with clarity, care, and confidence. This isn't the end. It's the beginning of your fluency.